Lieven Ameel, Jens Martin Gurr, Barbara Buchenau
Narrative in Urban Planning

Urban Studies

Lieven Ameel, born in 1978, is a senior lecturer in comparative literature at University of Tampere, Finland. He is co-founder and current president of the Association for Literary Urban Studies. In his research, he works on urban futures across textual genres, narrated experiences of space, and rhetorical structures in urban planning, among others.

Jens Martin Gurr, born in 1974, is a professor of British and Anglophone Literature and Culture at the University of Duisburg-Essen. He is cofounder and speaker of the Competence Field Metropolitan Research in the Universitätsallianz Ruhr (KoMet). His research areas include literary urban studies, theories and methods of urban and metropolitan research, model theory, literature and climate change as well as British literature of the 17th to the 21st centuries and contemporary US fiction.

Barbara Buchenau, born in 1968, is a professor of North American studies at Universität Duisburg-Essen, Germany, where she is heading the research group "Scripts for Postindustrial Urban Futures: American Models, Transatlantic Interventions", nicknamed *City Scripts*, funded by the VolkswagenFoundation, at the Universitätsallianz Ruhr (2018-2022). Her research is dedicated to the powerful alignments between literature and the land across the centuries.

Lieven Ameel, Jens Martin Gurr, Barbara Buchenau
Narrative in Urban Planning
A Practical Field Guide

[transcript]

The publication of this volume has been generously supported by the Volkswagen Foundation in the context of the Research Group "Scripts for Postindustrial Urban Futures: American Models, Transatlantic Interventions" (Az: 93500).

Bibliographic information published by the Deutsche Nationalbibliothek
The Deutsche Nationalbibliothek lists this publication in the Deutsche Nationalbibliografie; detailed bibliographic data are available in the Internet at http://dnb.d-nb.de

This work is licensed under the Creative Commons Attribution 4.0 (BY) license, which means that the text may be remixed, transformed and built upon and be copied and redistributed in any medium or format even commercially, provided credit is given to the author.
Creative Commons license terms for re-use do not apply to any content (such as graphs, figures, photos, excerpts, etc.) not original to the Open Access publication and further permission may be required from the rights holder. The obligation to research and clear permission lies solely with the party re-using the material.

First published in 2023 by transcript Verlag, Bielefeld
© Lieven Ameel, Jens Martin Gurr, Barbara Buchenau

Cover layout: Maria Arndt, Bielefeld
Cover illustration: Photo by Jens Martin Gurr
Printed by: Majuskel Medienproduktion GmbH, Wetzlar
https://doi.org/10.14361/9783839466179
Print-ISBN 978-3-8376-6617-5
PDF-ISBN 978-3-8394-6617-9
ISSN of series: 2747-3619
eISSN of series: 2747-3635

Printed on permanent acid-free text paper.

Contents

Acknowledgements 7

Sources 9

Introduction 13

Ambiguity 17

Closure 21

Emplotment 27

Future Narratives 33

Genre 39

Metaphor 45

Model 51

Narrative 57

Narrativity 63

Palimpsest 69

Path-dependency	73
Placemaking	79
Polyphony	85
Rhythm & Repetition	91
Scenario	95
Scripts	101
Travelling Models	107
Utopia	113
Works Cited	119
Notes	133

Acknowledgements

The ideas for this field guide took shape in discussions with several distinctive academic communities which helped us to clarify the specific need for a concise, hands-on manual for using narrative and storytelling in urban planning. First of all, we would like to thank the research group "Scripts for Postindustrial Urban Futures: American Models, Transatlantic Interventions" funded by the Volkswagen Foundation (2018–2023) – it has been a pleasure to work with Juliane Borosch, Florian Deckers, Kornelia Freitag, Walter Grünzweig, Randi Gunzenhäuser, Elisabeth Haefs, Chris Katzenberg, Johannes Krickl, Hanna Rodewald, Maria Sulimma, Michael Wala, and Katharina Wood on the multiple intersections between American studies and urban practice. In this research group, the work with our business partners in urban planning, urban development and urban art, most notably Diane van Buren and Ernest Zachary of Zachary & Associates in Detroit, Kai Lipsius of the Green Capital Agency, Essen, Thomas Rühle of Ökozentrum NRW in Hamm, Northrhine-Westfalia, Sebastian Schlecht of lala.ruhr and Bocafloja of the Quilomboarte Art Collective, has enriched our sense of the practical impact of narratives on urban practice.

We would also like to thank colleagues at Tampere University and Turku Institute for Advanced Studies (TIAS), as well as at the Association for Literary Urban Studies (ALUS). Our gratitude goes out to the inspiring environment provided by the YTK Land Use Planning and Urban Studies Group, Aalto University, Finland.

Further thanks go to the Competence Field "Metropolitan Research" in the University Alliance Ruhr, funded by Stiftung Mercator, and to numerous partner institutions for providing stimulating environments and for providing occasions to develop and test in practice some of the ideas for this book. We particularly wish to acknowledge the City of Essen and its Head of Environment, Traffic and Sports, Simone Raskob, as well as the Emschergenossenschaft and its Chairman Prof. Dr. Uli Paetzel.

We are grateful for discussions with the following colleagues: Stephanie Leigh Batiste, Julika Griem, Uta Hohn, Bart Keunen, Panu Lehtovuori, Paula M.L. Moya, Rolf Parr, J. Alexander Schmidt, Sofie Verraest, Hans-Werner Wehling and Thorsten Wiechmann.

And we would like to express our gratitude to the students who attended our various seminars, workshops and guest lectures about narratives in the context of planning – your genuine interest and questions have provided inspiration, food for thought, and important reference points for our work.

Sources

This book builds on our own long-standing research in historical as well as contemporary literary and cultural urban studies and in related fields. In the text, we draw on individual formulations, passages and examples from the following texts:

Ameel, Lieven. "A *bildungsroman* for a Waterfront Development: Literary Genre and the Planning Narratives of Jätkäsaari, Helsinki." *Journal of Urban Cultural Studies* 3, no. 2 (2016): 167–187.

Ameel, Lieven. "Cities Utopian, Dystopian and Apocalyptic." *Palgrave Handbook of Literature and the City*. Ed. Jeremy Tambling. London: Palgrave, 2016. 785–800.

Ameel, Lieven. "Emplotting Urban Regeneration: Narrative Strategies in the Case of Kalasatama, Helsinki." *Re-City. Future City – Combining Disciplines*. Ed. Juho Rajaniemi. DATUTOP 34 (2016): 223–241.

Ameel, Lieven. "Narrative Mapping and Polyphony in Urban Planning." *Yhdyskuntasuunnittelu / Finnish Journal for Urban Studies* 2 (2016): 20–40.

Ameel, Lieven. "Towards a Narrative Typology of Urban Planning Narratives for, in, and of Planning in Jätkäsaari, Helsinki." *Urban Design International* 22, no. 4 (2016): 318–330.

Ameel, Lieven. "Metaphorizations of the Waterfront in New York City's Comprehensive Waterfront Development Plan *Vision 2020* and Foer's 'The Sixth Borough.'" *Critique: Studies in Contemporary Fiction* 60, no. 3 (2019): 251–262.

Ameel, Lieven. "Governing the Future: Perspectives from Literary Studies – Commentary to Jones." *Fennia* 197, no. 1 (2019): 145–148.

Ameel, Lieven. "Fraught Fictionality in Narratives of Future Catastrophe." *Narrative* 29, no. 3 (2021): 355–373.

Ameel, Lieven. *The Narrative Turn in Urban Planning: Plotting the Helsinki Waterfront*. New York: Routledge, 2021.

Ameel, Lieven. "Redemptive Scripts in the City Novel." *City Scripts: Narratives of Postindustrial Urban Futures*. Ed. Barbara Buchenau, Jens Martin Gurr, Maria Sulimma. Columbus: Ohio State University Press, forthcoming.

Borosch, Juliane, Barbara Buchenau. "Walking Down Woodward – (Re-)Telling a City's Stories through Urban Figures." *City Scripts: Narratives of Postindustrial Urban Futures*. Ed. Barbara Buchenau, Jens Martin Gurr, Maria Sulimma. Columbus: Ohio State University Press, forthcoming.

Buchenau, Barbara, Jens Martin Gurr. "'Scripts' in Urban Development: Procedural Knowledge, Self-Description and Persuasive Blueprint for the Future." Jens Martin Gurr. *Charting Literary Urban Studies: Texts as Models of and for the City*. New York: Routledge, 2021. 141–163. https://doi.org/10.4324/9781003111009-8.

Buchenau, Barbara, Jens Martin Gurr. "On the Textuality of American Cities and their Others: A Disputation." *Projecting American Studies: Essays on Theory, Method, and Practice*. Ed. Frank Kelleter, Alexander Starre. Heidelberg: Winter, 2018. 135–152.

Buchenau, Barbara, Jens Martin Gurr. "Urban American Studies and the Conjunction of Textual Strategies and Spatial Processes." *Spaces—Communities—Representations: Urban Transformations in the USA*. Ed. Julia Sattler. Bielefeld: transcript, 2016. 395–420.

Buchenau, Barbara, Jens Martin Gurr, Maria Sulimma, eds. *City Scripts: Narratives of Postindustrial Urban Futures*. Columbus: Ohio State University Press, forthcoming.

Butler, Martin, Jens Martin Gurr. "Urbane Populärkultur als Bewertungspraxis und -ressource: Zum normativen Potential populärkultureller Inszenierung und diskursiver Aneignung urbaner Räume." *Place-Making in urbanen Diskursen*. Ed. Ingo H. Warnke, Beatrix Busse. Berlin/München/Boston: de Gruyter, 2014. 369–384.

Gurr, Jens Martin. *Charting Literary Urban Studies: Texts as Models of and for the City*. New York/London: Routledge, 2021. Open access: https://doi.org/10.4324/9781003111009.

Gurr, Jens Martin. "Palimpsest." *The Routledge Companion to Literary Urban Studies*. Ed. Lieven Ameel. New York/London: Routledge, 2022. 72–86.

Introduction

City planning thrives on future-oriented imagination and on visions of the possible city, created in dialogue with citizens as well as with policymakers. It is intimately bound up with forms of storytelling, so much so that planning has been defined in recent decades as inherently a narrative activity, a form of "persuasive storytelling", or even the act of city story-writing.[1] Planning is concerned with envisioning the future state of an individual plot of land, a neighbourhood or an entire district, and in its textual materials and policy texts, it will tend to describe the transition from a present-day state to this desired future state. More implicitly, through maps, digital 3D renderings or scaled physical models, it will evoke particular narrative frames with which to approach urban problems and their solutions. In literary studies, precisely this – the rendering of a change from situation A to situation B – is regarded as the kernel of any story. Whenever planners address city administrators, investors, inhabitants, and other stakeholders, they make use of the persuasive function of narrative. In doing so, they may appeal, for example, to a neighbourhood's or a district's past and thus to its sense of identity; and they will seek to tell a plausible story of how future developments can either be seen as building on that past or as promising a new start.

The insight that narrative is an essential part of planning has led to a considerable research literature by planning theorists, and even to a "narrative turn in urban planning".[2] But this narrative turn has not consistently entered planning practice. In our view, at least, it is rarely being used in a way that realizes the consequences of this insight. Planners, we argue, should be aware of the functions, effects and consequences of narratives for their practice: Specific narrative patterns can be powerful tools for persuasion, and will be beneficial for connecting future plans with past historical layers of meaning. Planners could be made more aware of the complex meaning-making functions, the ideological implications and the very real effects of particular narrative strategies. They should also be aware of the persuasive and potentially manipulative effects of narratives.

The term narrative has recently seen an inflationary use and is often uncritically employed in a wide range of fields (narrative economics and narrative change management are just two examples).[3] We therefore aim to identify, define, and illustrate key terms in the context of narrative and planning in a way that is grounded in rigorous research but that is also immediately applicable to particular planning contexts.

This book is a practical field guide to narrative aimed at planners, and written by three literary scholars. As literary scholars, in addition to our *research* on the role of narratives in planning, we have in various ways been involved in planning *practice*, training planning scholars and planning practitioners, collaborating with planners in interdisciplinary projects, or working on consulting projects that advised municipalities on how to harness the power of stories in urban development. What we set out to do is to make insights from narrative research accessible to planners; more precisely, we explain key concepts and terms that originate largely in literary studies and show how an awareness of the ways in which narratives work is directly relevant for planners. In deliberately focusing on eighteen central terms and concepts, we do not attempt any kind of exhaustive inventory nor a planning history, but a practical glossary of key concepts in the field of narrative in planning. Both in the choice of terms and concepts and in each individual entry, we focus on usability and applicability: What do planners need to know in order to use narrative approaches responsibly in their practice? What makes narratives coherent, effective, probable, persuasive, even individually and collectively necessary – but also potentially harmful, manipulative and divisive? How can narratives help build more sustainable, resilient, and inclusive communities?

This book should be useful to anyone who is working on the intersection between the built environment and the world as it is conceived, imagined and debated. Taking our cue mostly from terms originating in literary studies and exploring their reach in the field of planning, we also aim to reach literary scholars working on real-world problems or seeking to apply their insights in what has often come to be called third-mission projects, outreach, or community engagement projects. One other possible audience consists of humanities scholars who wish to train students with an eye to fields of employment outside academia and the teaching profession. We therefore hope this book may also be of use as a first stepping stone for undergraduate or graduate students.

In part, the idea for this book developed in reaction to an increasing proliferation of storytelling terminology in fields outside of literary studies. It is not inspired by any desire to reclaim a terminology, but is spurred on, rather, by the need to bring together interdisciplinary theory and everyday practice around robust academic research, combining theoretical rigour with hands-on applicability.

This is not merely a matter of an insistence on precise terminology. Narratives shape perceptions and perceptions shape reality – think of investment decisions or residential preferences: If a neighbourhood is often enough represented as being unsafe, people may not want to live there or buy property there; the same, of course, is true of travel choices. Moreover, narrative not only persuasively *conveys* knowledge, it also *shapes* and even *produces* knowledge. Form and content are inseparable in stories: Narrative patterns and metaphors are not chosen to decorate the story once it is there, they do not come on top of a plan or garnish it – rather, they fundamentally contribute to the meaning of a story. Every narrative is unique: when a story is told in different ways, by using different plot patterns or central images, the result is a different kind of narrative with different functions and effects.[4]

Finally, the global diffusion of influential concepts and blueprints for urban development – from Ebenezer Howard's 'Garden City' to today's 'Smart City' – is not best explained by how well such concepts respond to urban challenges; rather, the popular success of such travelling models is often better explained by the way they are successfully framed by means of compelling narratives.[5] As has been shown for the 'Smart City', for instance, this can largely be regarded as an instance of "corporate storytelling".[6] If urban planning is essentially a story-telling activity, urban planners and students of urban planning and architecture will need expertise in storytelling. This book will provide them with practical definitions, examples, and directions for further applications.

Our deliberately selective list of key terms can broadly be grouped into three categories: (1) a majority of terms that originate in literary studies and that have been or might be used to make sense of urban problems (terms such as narrative, emplotment, genre); (2) conversely, a smaller number of terms that are primarily applied to urban phenomena but that gain depth if supplemented by a literary studies perspective (terms such as path-dependency or place-making); (3) terms that are widely used in a broad range of fields, if frequently with different meanings (terms such as model, or scenario).

Each entry provides a brief definition of the term, an example, a brief explanation of the concept including its origins and key implications, a discussion of potential further applications, a list of related entries, and a few very selective suggestions for further reading. In our choice of examples, we do not seek to be representative or to cover the broadest possible range of different cities; rather, we draw on some of the examples we know best from our own research, such as Antwerp, the German Ruhr region, Helsinki, and New York City.

The entries are self-contained and can be read individually, and this book is primarily meant to serve as a reference work. But the entries can also be read in sequence, and, taken together, they provide an overview of key terms and concepts from the field and may, we hope, serve alike planning practitioners and literary scholars with a view to real-world applications.

Ambiguity

1. Definition

Ambiguity may be defined as the phenomenon of a term, an utterance, a text, an image or a concept having several meanings or potential interpretations, the Greek "ambi-" root strictly speaking suggesting exactly two meanings.

2. Example

At the simplest level, many common words in everyday language are ambiguous, words like "set" or "bank" (both as nouns and as verbs) being obvious examples. Visually, the so-called Necker cube (see fig. 1) is a well-known example: It is unclear whether we are looking at the cube from above or from below.

Fig. 1: Necker cube; source: Daniel Bläser, www.dbgrafik.de

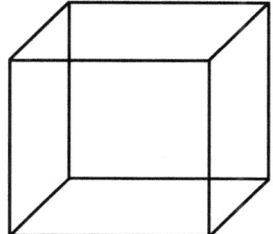

3. Explanation

Ambiguity may arise at several levels and may have several causes: Thus, we might distinguish – at least – between verbal, syntactic and semantic or conceptual ambiguity. Moreover, ambiguity needs to be distinguished from related terms such as ambivalence or contradiction, which, although frequently treated as overlapping concepts or even as synonymous, should be regarded as different categories from diverse fields of intellectual inquiry. While ambivalence is originally a psychological or cognitive concept designating a state of indecision, undecidability or unclear evaluation, contradiction is a notion from logic designating two or more irreconcilable propositions. Ambiguity, by contrast, is originally a rhetorical concept, refering to the simultaneous presence of more than one possible meaning or interpretation. Ambiguity in a text may be the *result* of attitudinal ambivalence, which manifests itself in unresolved contradictions in the text. But ambiguity is just as much a result of an act of observation and its accompanying sense of uncertainty and multiplicity. In any longer document, ambiguity may also be the result of a sequence of propositions which, each in themselves, are unambiguous but irreconcilable with one another. Even if any individual passage is perfectly clear, the unharmonized concatenation of contradictory passages, as its cumulative effect, may still create an ambiguity of the text as a whole. This sequential type of ambiguity may be the result of ambivalent attitudes on the part of one author, but it may also be the result of an unsuccessful attempt at harmonizing or combining a plenitude of interests. In a more positive sense, however, ambiguity does not have to be seen as the *result* of an imprecise use of language. Rather, language, and especially literary language, often allows for the resolution, suspension, or sublation – one might more critically also speak of the glossing over – of a multiplicity of possible meanings or of contradictions in a type of deliberate ambiguity.

While, in planning theory, there is a substantial discussion about issues of complexity, this is hardly the case with ambiguity. In the few contributions that exist, ambiguity generally appears as a problem to be solved.[7] Where related terms such as (un)certainty, flexibility and fuzziness rather than ambiguity are used in planning debates, in each case, it seems, there are conflicts of interest with regard to the openness as opposed to determinacy of planning policies, regulations and individual plans. Here, too, there is a tendency to regard ambiguity as ultimately problematic.

4. Applications

Think of the various living labs that have been sprouting up on the campuses of universities in the past decade: at Stanford, urban researchers meet with stakeholders – citizens, farmers, businesspeople and politicians – to experiment with and discuss a variety of scenarios to deal with water scarcity in Amman and Pune. In Amsterdam, partners from research institutions as well as the private and the public sector jointly seek to develop small-scale solutions to wicked urban problems.[8] In both cases, there is plenty of ambiguity concerning the roles, the authority and the leverage of all of the actors involved, and a great part of the challenge of these labs is the effective management of this ambiguity. While most professions – law, medicine, technology, planning – will generally seek to eliminate or at least to minimize ambiguity, scholars of narrative have argued that ambiguity may also foster social cohesion: By accepting "doubt and plurality or plenty [as] the twin poles of ambiguity", by allowing more diverse groups of stakeholders to find points of identification but also contention, narratives attain a certain fuzziness and indeterminacy.[9] These ambiguity-tolerant narratives leave room for interpretation, for adverse readings and for negotiation; precisely because of this communal interpretive work involved they are *more* rather than *less* socially binding than precise narratives, and thus *more* conducive to generating social cohesion and to canvassing public support.[10] A classic case in point would be programmes of political parties, which, if too specific, could hardly generate broad support across different societal groups and coalitions of interest.

Thus, while one will hardly want to suggest that planning documents – let alone legal texts or contracts – should deliberately be ambiguous, it may be helpful to bear in mind this social function of ambiguity. Not only is the tolerance of ambiguity a central ability for individuals to function in complex, highly differentiated social environments. Ambiguous documents – or those which allow different stakeholders complementary, possibly even contradictory means of identification and interpretation – may productively function as "boundary objects", objects or frames of knowledge which are flexible enough to be adopted by different communities.[11]

Related entries: Closure, Future Narratives, Metaphor, Scenario

Further Reading

Forester, John. *Critical Theory, Public Policy, and Planning Practice: Towards a Critical Pragmatism*. Albany: State University of New York Press, 1993.

Gurr, Jens Martin. *Charting Literary Urban Studies: Texts as Models of and for the City*. New York/London: Routledge, 2021.

Rittel, Horst W. J., Melvin M. Webber. "Dilemmas in a General Theory of Planning." *Policy Sciences* 4, no. 2 (1973). 155–169.

Sharp, Darren, Rob Raven. "Urban Planning by Experiment at Precinct Scale: Embracing Complexity, Ambiguity, and Multiplicity." *Urban Planning* 6, no. 1 (2021). DOI: https://doi.org/10.17645/up.v6i1.3525.

Closure

1. Definition

Closure is the resolution, in the ending of a story, of the conflicts and tensions described. When a story has closure, a perceived imbalance is restored; a difficulty is finally overcome; good or evil get their rewards. Closure is what gives a meaning and a purpose to all that has preceded it; it gives a story a sense of completeness, and as such, it is closely bound up with why readers or listeners are compelled and moved – also affectively – by stories. Closure ensures that the expectations of the reader, raised in the course of the narration, are satisfied. While closure is the expected norm in literature and everyday storytelling, there are any number of stories that deny the reader or listener a satisfying ending. In the context of planning, closure relates not only to the ending of a planning narrative, but also to how a proposed plan can provide a sense of closure after urban degeneration or periods of tensions between competing interests in a city.

2. Example

The twenty-first century plans for the redevelopment of the Antwerp Quays (2010) are constructed around providing closure to a story in which the conflicting interests had for too long been unresolved, to the dissatisfaction of the public. The Quays, located near the city centre along the right bank of the Scheldt, 6,8km long and roughly 100m in width, had been left neglected for decades, separating the city from the water. Potentially prime real estate was used for parking – the "most beautiful car parking space in Europe".[12] In the master plan for the Scheldt Quays, the redeveloping of the Quays balances the legacy of the post-industrial waterfront with the demands of rising water levels to restore the connection between the river and the city. Not only the quays, but also the city is described as achieving a degree of completeness as the result of the plan. The example is typical of a plan visualizing the moment of closure when an imbalance is restored or a conflict resolved. An interesting twist – found in a range of similar post-industrial waterfront developments – is that the narrative closure tends to coincide with an opening up of the urban public space to a public that had only limited access to these sites, from the industrial era onward. Narrative closure tends to presuppose that the end-state has been preordained, or is somehow natural or inevitable, which is one of the reasons why closure can lend a powerful rhetoric to policy narratives. The plans for the Antwerp Quays (see fig. 2) emphasize that the plans return to the citizens and the city what is rightfully theirs, enabling the city to fulfil part of its natural destiny as a city defined by the river.[13]

Fig. 2: Visualisation of the Zuidersluis, Antwerp Quays. Source: © PROAP and City of Antwerp, 2011

3. Explanation

Closure is the ending that gives meaning to all that has come before. In classical tragedy and comedy, the final scene is what decides whether a play will be a tragedy (ending tragically) or a comedy (ending well). A meaningful ending is not only the expected norm – although not necessarily upheld – of many literary texts, but of all forms of narrative: closure is akin to the closing statements in everyday conversations, a way to wrap up what has been told, but also to summarise its meaning and relevance.[14] In classical rhetorics, closure is what enables an artwork to be complete and wholesome, and hence both convincing and aesthetically pleasing. In everyday storytelling and also in literary texts, closure is associated with the final utterings of narration. Planning texts in many ways operate quite differently – nobody expects people to read planning documents from end to end – and it is more productive to think of the plan itself as providing closure to a storyline that is set out in the course of planning documents.

In postmodern theory, closure has generally become suspect. Closure was deemed to be aligned with the ideologically flawed "great narratives" and the power structures they upheld; the very rhetorical compulsiveness and effectiveness of closure is also what Marxist and feminist scholars objected to. There have always been narratives that deliberately deny the reader or listener clear closure, but in the postmodern area, a deliberate refusal of closure has become part of the dominant mode of storytelling.

In planning theory, an aligned evolution away from great narratives and from comprehensive end-plans can be found in the shift from rational planning theory to more incremental planning practices. Recent thinking in planning theory and practice has increasingly emphasized the need to plan for uncertainty, and the importance of flexible and reversible planning. Seeing planning in terms of narrative closure and open-endedness provides one important approach towards those aims.

4. Applications

Telling a story that convincingly moves towards closure can be one way to add rhetorical power to a narrative in planning, and to convince the public, private-public partnerships, or various stakeholders, of the causal logic of particular decisions. But open-ended narratives in planning may have other benefits. When the borders of closure are drawn too rigidly, this may impede future adjustments to new challenges and be a check on the resilience and flexibility of a city. Stories have endings, but reality does not – and real-world cities never finish the process of transformation and adaptation. Planning narratives that are open-ended leave more room to envision alternative possibilities or future change, and more space for the agency of communities or individual citizens. In concrete terms, planning without closure would mean the inclusion of multiple alternative endings, allowing for a degree of multi-voicedness or polyphony; it would entail the explicit acknowledgement of doubts, ambiguities and uncertainties, and the incorporation of deliberate contradictions and gaps in planning texts and their visualizations. Such approaches are arguably already used to some extent in nonbinding strategic planning, and are one area in which urban planning can learn from informal spatial planning.[15]

Related entries: Emplotment, Future Narratives, Path-dependency, Polyphony, Scenario

Further Reading

Abbott, H. Porter. "Closure." *Routledge Encyclopedia of Narrative Theory*. Ed. David Herman, Manfred Jahn, Marie-Laure Ryan. London: Routledge, 2010. 65–66.

Ameel, Lieven. "Redemptive Scripts in the City Novel." *City Scripts: Narratives of Postindustrial Urban Futures*. Ed. Barbara Buchenau, Jens Martin Gurr, Maria Sulimma. Columbus: Ohio State University Press, forthcoming.

Antwerp. *Tussen stad en stoom. Het Masterplan Scheldekaaien Antwerpen.* Antwerp: City of Antwerp, 2011.

Kermode, Frank. *The Sense of an Ending: Studies in the Theory of Fiction.* London: Oxford University Press, 1967.

Emplotment

1. Definition

Emplotment is the act of situating events, characters, and places into a plot, a sequence of events in space and time.[16] In the context of planning, emplotment plays on the double meaning of the word plot, which denotes both a spatial location and the development of a story.

2. Example

In the New York comprehensive waterfront plan *Vision 2020*, the opening pages of this 180-odd page document introduce the planning area and the plans, and in doing so, situate place and plan within a distinctive plot that emphasizes the redressing of past wrongs and a renewed balance between a variety of interests. The introductory chapter of *Vision 2020* sets the tone:

> After decades of turning our backs on the shoreline—allowing it to devolve into a no-man's land of rotting piers, parking lots, and abandoned industrial sites—New York made reclamation of the waterfront a priority.[17]

With these words, the planning area is situated not only geographically, but also as part of a distinct narrative plot, in which the New York shoreline has fallen from grace but will be reclaimed and restored, previous wrongs will be righted, and imbalances adjusted. Several elements that support this mode of emplotment are outlined in the Introduction of the plan, as well as in its two prefaces. The shoreline is described repeatedly as one of the "most important resources" and "assets" of New York; its inclusion and restoration is enacted also by the coining of new metaphors, such as the idea of the "Blue Network", a concept introduced in the plan to denote the waterways of New York. The outcome will be beneficial in many ways, as is asserted throughout the text: "Reconnecting with the water will provide social, economic, and environmental advantages."[18] Emplotment means situating this development area, the plan, and the argumentation for particular decisions, within a broader narrative of historical neglect and reclamation of what is lost; of resolution and redemption. The resulting effect is a causal and rational drive for the decisions laid out in the plan (see fig. 3).

Fig. 3: *The New York waterfront at Williamsburg, Brooklyn, with Domino's Factory redevelopment. Image by Lieven Ameel. October 2019*

3. Explanation

In appearance and purpose, planning and policy documents are obviously very different from single-author novels. But all planning narratives exhibit some thematic, linguistic and stylistic features that situate the planning area on a geographical map *and* within a narrative pattern. Emplotment is the narrative strategy that situates a specific event or events within a larger narrative framework, giving sense, structure, coherence and causality to what otherwise would remain a mere enumeration of actions.

The use of emplotment as a narrative concept outside the field of literary studies is associated with the work of Hayden White and his examination of historiographical texts in terms of their narrative. White used "emplotment" to denote the processes by which events are contextualized into meaning-making totalities, receiving "the formal coherency that only stories can possess".[19] He distinguishes four modes of emplotment: romance, tragedy, comedy and satire. The difference between these different modes is in world-view and in how these narratives find their completion. Romance – the kind of story associated with knights on a quest – tends to revolve around a hero's accomplishments and the overcoming of obstacles; "a drama of the triumph of good over evil, of virtue over vice, of light over darkness ..."[20] Satire has an opposing worldview, in which the main character is unable to overcome the obstacles created by the world or society; it questions notions of societal unity and the possibility of happy resolution. The difference between tragedy and comedy is not so much in their worldview, but primarily in their ending: In its resolution, comedy resolves tensions and ends with reconciliations – the happy ending of marriage or new beginnings. Tragedy ends with disaster (most, though not all, Greek tragedies are a case in point), but the worldview in tragedy does not have to be hopeless, since the readers or onlookers of tragedy may have gained some new knowledge about the world, and about their place within it. Emplotment is one of the ways in which narratives interact with readers' expectations, since it is designed to activate and structure readers' preconceived knowledge and their horizon of expectation, and to draw on the kind of dominant scripts and frames of knowledge that narratively structure experience. In planning theory, Hayden White's examination of narrative tropes within historiography has been applied in re-examining planning histories.[21] Its usefulness for an analysis of urban planning has been illustrated by Mareile Walter's examination of narratives of Swedish Karlskrona.[22] Walter draws on White's theory of emplotment to show that Karlskrona's *Översiktsplan 2030* is structured as a "comedy of the sustainable city". In the example from the planning of the New York waterfront that introduced this entry, the emplotment follows the romantic and the comic mode, in which the planners and the city are seen as heroes who overcome monumental difficulties to reach their goal and to triumph over past wrongs (romantic mode), and providing a happy ending in which seemingly contradictory interests become balanced and resolved (comic mode).

As has become apparent, plot endings are defining elements in emplotment, since they provide a measure of closure and are thus central for attributing meaning and value to what is recounted. Beginnings are equally important, setting the stage for how an area will be presented in narrative terms. In planning texts, the opening paragraphs and the conclusions are the most obvious places to find narrative elements that emplot the development area as well as the plan itself.

4. Applications

Drawing on emplotment in the context of planning means to be particularly aware of how beginnings and endings set the tone not only for the spatial contextualization of a development area, but also for the kinds of narrative scripts, frames, and expectations that are activated within the reader. Beginnings of a planning text can deliberately set the stage for a narrative of recovery by starting out with a historical description of neglect, as happens in the example from the New York waterfront. Drawing on particular metaphors from the area's cultural history can lend further rhetorical power to such modes of emplotment. But it is important to be aware that powerful beginnings and the particular modes of emplotment can raise unrealistic expectations or lead to path-dependency that at worst could limit flexibility for future plans.

Related entries: Closure, Genre, Path-dependency, Scripts

Further Reading

Ameel, Lieven. "Emplotting Urban Regeneration: Narrative Strategies in the Case of Kalasatama, Helsinki." *Re-City. Future City – Combining Disciplines.* Ed. Juho Rajaniemi. *DATUTOP* 34 (2016): 223–241.

Ryan, Marie-Laure. "Narrative in Real Time: Chronicle, Mimesis and Plot in the Baseball Broadcast." *Narrative* 1, no. 2 (1993): 138–155.

van Hulst, Merlijn, Haridimos Tsoukas. "Understanding Extended Narrative Sensemaking: How Police Officers Accomplish Story Work." *Organization* (July 3, 2021). Online first. https://doi.org/10.1177/13505084211026878.

Future Narratives

1. Definition

A future narrative[23] is a narrative that describes an event or experience that is set – when seen from the perspective of actual writing – in a moment of time in the future. A future narrative does not – as most narratives do – present a development as having already happened in the past and thus as no longer allowing for different outcomes. Rather, future narratives portray the future as being open and subject to intervention. A future narrative tends to establish a relationship between the real world (at the time of writing or narrating) and the world described in the future narrative on the basis of a measure of continuation, with possible pathways to the narrated future implied or explicitly outlined. A future narrative contains decision points at which different future developments are possible; these decision points are referred to as "nodes".

2. Example

Since planning is both naturally future-oriented and inherently narrative, any planning document refers to at least one possible future, and contains – explicitly or implicitly – at least one node to connect the future storyworld to the real world at the time of writing. Any plan for the future is essentially a future narrative, because even where the end-state is presented as a necessary outcome without alternatives, the plan contains – at least implicitly – the decision point of realization or non-realization. In the simplest form – and this is perhaps even the most common form – the alternatives may only be that a plan is either realized or not realized. In more fully developed form, plans for the future development of an area often explicitly present city councilors, investors, voters, and other stakeholders with two or more options between which a decision must be made. In particular in the case of informal planning practices, including scenario workshops or non-binding strategic plans, multiple future narratives can be included.

The example (see fig. 4), published in 2019, envisions how a child born at the time of publication will see their world in 2050. Events are described in the present tense ("New York ... is no longer reliant on fossil fuels"), but there are elements that explicitly refer back to the base line of 2019 ("New modes of transportation" – as opposed to the ones in use at the time of writing), or that more implicitly outline the challenges at the moment of publication (e.g., "Safe, affordable housing is available in all five boroughs ...").[24]

3. Explanation

Merlijn van Hulst has drawn attention to the "future-directedness" of both narrative and planning: "Through telling and listening to stories, actors in the present not only make sense of the past, but also prepare for the future. This 'future-directedness', the imagination that is part of or that is enabled by stories, is especially relevant for practices such as planning."[25] This conception is close to the notion of "future narratives" as developed by literary scholar Christoph Bode in order to distinguish them from the more common form of "past narratives", which present events as having unfolded already and thus as no longer subject to intervention. Even grammatically, it should be noted, most narratives are formulated in the past tense. In future narratives, the fact that the future is open and subject to intervention is made explicit in the form of decision points or "nodes" in the narrative, which can either simply be bifurcations or may offer three or more alternatives. Each of these potential paths into the future can then, in turn, contain further nodes.

Fig. 4: *A Vision of New York City in 2050.*

A VISION OF NEW YORK CITY IN 2050

New York City will be a very different place in the middle of the 21st century. How will a child born today experience that future? Let's take a look.

IN 2050, NEW YORK CITY HAS MORE THAN 9 MILLION RESIDENTS.

The streets are bustling with people of all nationalities – some were born here, some are visitors, and some have chosen to make their home here. More than a million more flow into the city every day to work and explore the city's culture and neighborhoods. A dramatic skyline, bridges, and iconic buildings rise from world-famous islands and waterways. And there's a familiar, palpable sense of dynamism and creativity — people are in a hurry to accomplish great things.

IN 2050, NEW YORK CITY IS PREPARED FOR A CHANGING CLIMATE, AND IS NO LONGER RELIANT ON FOSSIL FUELS.

Buildings, transportation, and our economy are powered by renewable energy — wind, solar, and hydropower — through a modern, fully electric grid. We can't avoid every impact of climate change, but our infrastructure, public services, and residents are protected from the ravages of extreme weather. Every New Yorker benefits from these changes, which were undertaken in a fair way, and our adapted city is a model for the world to follow.

IN 2050, NEW YORKERS NO LONGER RELY ON CARS.

Our streets are safe and easy to navigate, reclaimed for people. Subways and buses are fast and reliable, taking people where they need to go and connecting our city to the wider metropolitan region. Bicycle lanes abound and walking is a favorite way of getting around town. For many New Yorkers, the daily commute to work is a scenic ferry ride. New modes of transportation, enabled by technology and responsibly deployed, add to the mobility options throughout the five boroughs.

IN 2050, NEW YORKERS ARE SECURE IN THEIR HOMES AND NEIGHBORHOODS.

Safe, affordable housing is available in all five boroughs, and our neighborhoods are more diverse and dynamic than ever. Communities are safe, the air and water are clean, and there are abundant open spaces for all to enjoy. In every neighborhood, there are cultural centers and libraries, small businesses and corner groceries open for late night shopping. No longer threatened by harassment or eviction, families can choose to raise their children in the neighborhoods that best meet their needs.

IN 2050, NEW YORK CITY'S ECONOMIC STRENGTH PROVIDES SECURITY AND OPPORTUNITY FOR ALL.

All New Yorkers can find a good job with fair wages, benefits, and the chance to advance. Young people, trained to think critically and ready to learn new skills, excel in their work and easily find jobs in a diversified and evolving economy. From big businesses to local start-ups, in manufacturing, technology, creative industries, New Yorkers are entrepreneurial and open to new opportunities, driving a growing economy in which everyone can take part and be rewarded.

IN 2050, HEALTH CARE IS A RIGHT FOR EVERY NEW YORKER.

New Yorkers are healthy because quality health care is guaranteed, and our holistic approach means healthy lifestyles — good nutrition, clean air, nearby parks — are available to everyone regardless of race, gender, ethnicity, or disability. New mothers, seniors, children with asthma, people struggling with substance misuse or mental illness — all have access to care and treatment across the five boroughs. New Yorkers interact regularly with their natural environment through an extensive network of trails and waterfront greenways.

Source: The City of New York: *OneNYC 2050. Building a Strong and Fair City*. p. 6. OneNYC 2050, Volume 1, April 2019. © City of New York. All rights reserved. Used with permission of the City of New York

Future narratives can also be approached drawing on the work of Bertrand de Jouvenel – one of the founding fathers of futures studies – for whom future narratives stand apart from the dichotomy fact/fiction, because they are concerned with a separate category: *futura*, or future facts.[26] Future narratives, crucially, do not have truth-value in the actual world at the time of their writing. But they may differ greatly in the degree of urgency with which they describe a possible future to its actual readership. If the audience contemporary with the time of publication is envisioned as being able to influence the future storyworld – as in New York City's strategy *OneNYC 2050* – future narratives have a particularly high degree of urgency.

4. Applications

In the practice of legally binding urban planning, plans – whether they are master plans for an entire district or plans for an individual building – generally do not explicitly present alternatives. However, in order to do justice to the fact that planning in democratic societies should never pretend to be without alternatives, but also in order to give stakeholders a sense of involvement, planning might benefit from explicitly formulating alternatives. In this way, planning could work with a limited number of scenarios fleshed out in brief narrative descriptions and suggestive visualizations. These ideally come with considerations on anticipated costs, benefits, environmental impact assessments and other relevant discussions of opportunities and threats.

Related entries: Closure, Narrative, Path-dependency, Scenario, Scripts

Further Reading

Ameel, Lieven. "Fraught Fictionality in Narratives of Future Catastrophe." *Narrative* 29, no. 3 (2021): 355–73.

Keunen, Bart. "Learning from Stories: Narrative Imagination in Urbanism." *Writingplace: Investigations in Architecture and Literature.* Ed. Klaske Havik, Jorge Mejía Hernández, Mike Schäfer, Mark

Proosten, Susana Oliveira. Rotterdam: nai010 Publishers, 2016. 18–33.

Meifert-Menhard, Felicitas. *Playing the Text, Performing the Future. Future Narratives in Print and Digiture.* Berlin/Boston: de Gruyter, 2013.

Genre

1. Definition

Literary genre is a type of literature defined by a distinct form, style, and aims. Genre can either mean a historical genre (such as the 1930s-50s hard-boiled detective novel), or a more general category, such as the genres of poetry, prose, and drama. Genres act as important "storehouses of cultural knowledge and possibility" and as "frameworks of expectation"; as such, they are crucial for guiding the reader's expectations and interpretations.[27] Textual genres also include non-fictional genres, such as the travel novel, the diary entry, or the memoir. The explanatory sections of urban plans can be seen as one textual genre with relatively rigid features in terms of form, style and aim, with specific genre conventions dependent on local and legal context.

2. Example

In 2009, the city of Helsinki published a literary novel it had commissioned from the author Hannu Mäkelä to promote Jätkäsaari, a post-industrial harbour development that was then under construction. The novel, entitled *Hyvä jätkä* (literally, 'good chap'), is distributed to all new inhabitants of the area. It describes a young working-class man's coming-of-age story in Helsinki around the turn of the twentieth century, and is a typical example of the genre of the *Bildungsroman*, or novel of development (see fig. 5). At the centre of the *Bildungsroman* is a young man (or woman) from provincial backgrounds who moves to the city to fulfil their potential and to achieve maturity. After inevitable setbacks and disappointments, the protagonist achieves their aims and is (re)integrated into society. Drawing its name from the German word for education ("Bildung"), the *Bildungsroman* is about bourgeois education, in which both the protagonist and the civil society benefit from upwardly mobile processes of integration. The reader, too, is part of these processes: in its prototypical form, the *Bildungsroman* is a literary genre that is meant to educate the reader.

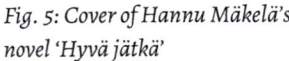

Fig. 5: Cover of Hannu Mäkelä's novel 'Hyvä jätkä'

In *Hyvä jätkä*, all these elements of the literary genre are visibly present: the protagonist, Johannes, achieves a slow development from a poor fisherman's son to becoming a self-taught construction worker and baker's boy, capacities in which he literally constructs and feeds the rapidly modernizing Finnish capital. The development of Johannes goes hand in hand with that of Helsinki, until both achieve a degree of independence: the novel ends just before 1917, when Finland became independent. And with the help of the book, the reader is educated on the historical development of the area of Jätkäsaari, which was transformed in the early decades of the twentieth century from a small community of fishers and holidaymakers, on the fringes of the city, to an industrial harbour. In its epilogue, the book connects this history to the future of the area, and educates the reader not only about the past but also on how the city planners are shaping the future of the city.

Perhaps surprisingly, the planning texts that describe urban plans for Jätkäsaari (more specifically, the partial local master plans) and that were published around the same time as *Hyvä jätkä*, contain several features of the genre of the *Bildungsroman*. Most importantly, they project the development of the area as the integration of a marginalized character into the natural urban fold of the city centre, in a process of mutually beneficial development. The urban development, planning documents claim, will not only sustain the existing urban balance; it will reverse a negative evolution, countering the earlier decline in numbers of inhabitants in the Helsinki peninsula during the preceding decades, and "increase the vitality of the city centre and improve the conditions for the development of the city".[28] And like the *Bildungsroman*, these planning texts aim not only to describe development, but to actively educate the reader. The lengthy explanatory sections of the planning documents can be seen as texts written to transform the reader towards a more responsible, cosmopolitan citizen with a better understanding of urbanity and urban development.

3. Explanation

The history of urban planning is closely interconnected with the history of particular literary genres. One literary genre with relevance is that of utopia, especially in the case of nineteenth-century utopias such as Edward Bellamy's *Looking Backward: 2000–1887* (1888) and E. Everett Hale's *Sybaris* (1869), books that proposed future urban forms to tackle the problems of industrialization and modernization, and that were influential also in planning circles.[29] There is a fascinating relationship between the development of urban planning as a discipline in this period and the spread of literary utopia.

It is important to note that specific genres come with specific expectations and with ideological baggage. The *Bildungsroman*, for example, has been seen as the "'symbolic form' of modernity"[30], and it has a special relation to optimistic views towards rationality, progress, the development of the middle class, and accelerating processes of modernization and industrialization. It is a genre that envisions a wholesome individual in harmony with a wholesome society, a vision that was reflected in enlightenment visions of a harmonious spatial environment that could lead to a well-educated citizen able to maximize his or her contribution to society.[31] After a promising start in the late eighteenth century, the prototypical *Bildungsroman* quickly fell out of fashion in the course of the nineteenth century, with literature instead focusing on characters that failed in their aims to integrate into society. In the course of the twentieth century, decolonizing movements also targeted the *Bildungsroman* as a quintessentially Eurocentric text form, and new genres such as the Black Bildungsroman draw on the genre features of the novel of development to move in new directions. In this context, it is remarkable that urban planners continue to use features borrowed (wittingly or not) from the genre of the *Bildungsroman* to describe and legitimate plans, with such features including the integration of a marginal entity into the larger urban fold, and the gradual development of a wholesome society, in which also the reader of the document finds education.

4. Applications

Consciously or unconsciously, all longer narrative texts make use of scripts and narrative genres to organize their material into a meaningful form. For planners, an awareness of genre opens up multiple opportunities. Genre is important in guiding readerly expectations, and a conscious use of genre features can be a powerful rhetorical and communicative strategy. Citizens and stakeholders can also be made more aware of the generic properties of planning texts, which are often (for practical as well as legal reasons) very rigid in their structure, style and narrative progression. Since many genres from literature and popular culture are instantly recognizable and may evoke powerful associations, literary genres could also be used to invite stakeholder feedback or to organize collaborative workshops – would it be possible to invite written feedback or citizens' input concerning urban development in the form of a haiku, a sonnet, a diary entry; and what kind of place-based knowledge would be generated in this way? More generally, a greater awareness of the genre of planning texts, and how these communicate with other kinds of textual genres, may be helpful in moving to more complex, more multi-voiced, and more open-ended forms of narrative planning.

Related entries: Narrative, Narrativity, Path-Dependency, Scenario

Further Reading

Ameel, Lieven. "A *bildungsroman* for a Waterfront Development: Literary Genre and the Planning Narratives of Jätkäsaari, Helsinki." *Journal of Urban Cultural Studies* 3, no. 2 (2016): 167–187.

Fowler, Alastair. *Kinds of Literature: An Introduction to the Theory of Genres and Modes*. Oxford: Oxford University Press, 1982.

LeSeur, Geta J. *Ten is the Age of Darkness: The Black Bildungsroman*. Columbia: University of Missouri Press, 1995.

Metaphor

1. Definition

Metaphor is the transfer of meaning from a word's usual context to a new one. Typically, a metaphor takes the form of a comparison without explicitly saying "x is similar to y". The transfer of meaning from one domain to another is not entirely random, but nevertheless provides a sense of the unexpected: it tends to happen according to an internal logic, for example when a pig is used to denote someone with bad eating habits; or a can of sardines to denote cramped living quarters.

2. Example

In the New York City comprehensive waterfront plan *Vision 2020*, the idea of a new engagement with the water and the waterfront, after decades of neglect, is crystallized in a compelling metaphor: that of the New York water as a "Sixth Borough." It is a conceptualization introduced in the preface by the Commissioner, Amanda Burden:

> Our water is the connective tissue between our boroughs and is, in effect, our Sixth Borough.[32]

The metaphor was used repeatedly in various presentations of the plan and was quickly picked up by the media. The idea of a "Sixth Borough" is relatively well-known among inhabitants of New York City. It posits the existence of an imagined sixth community or locality in addition to the five established boroughs. Examples of this usage include references to New Yorkers' holiday or retirement community in Florida, or the commuters from New Jersey who work in New York, or the prison population on Rikers Island as imagined "sixth boroughs." By giving New York's waterscape the name of "Sixth Borough," *Vision 2020* and the media coverage of the plan use metaphor to enable New Yorkers to see their water in a new light.

3. Explanation

Metaphors are crucial rhetorical strategies that have been studied and consciously applied at least since early antiquity. Metaphors are also crucial ways for structuring our knowledge about our position in the world. Ideas like "life as a road", or "up" and "down" as shorthand for "good" or "bad", are effectively "metaphors we live by".[33] In that sense, metaphors are akin to scripts: they are a structural narrative form that informs how we see the world and that defines our possibilities to speak of our future selves.

Stories in planning and policy texts tend to be constructed around "generative metaphors" that link "casual accounts of policy problems to particular proposals for action" and that connect "accounts of 'is' and 'ought'".[34] Some of the most powerful metaphors to imagine urban relationships, such as that of the city as body, or the more recent metaphor of city as "resilient" or "smart" draw on imagined analogies with the human body or the natural world. What such metaphors do is posit, in condensed form, a city problem and its solution in a way that suggests compelling causal relationships. If the city is said to be "congested", the logical solution that presents itself is new infrastructure for better circulation. Metaphors in planning are not external to the material city; rather, they are central to how problems and their solutions are imagined and formulated, and to how cities' material morphology is framed and shaped.

Fig. 6: Copenhagen Finger Plan (1974)

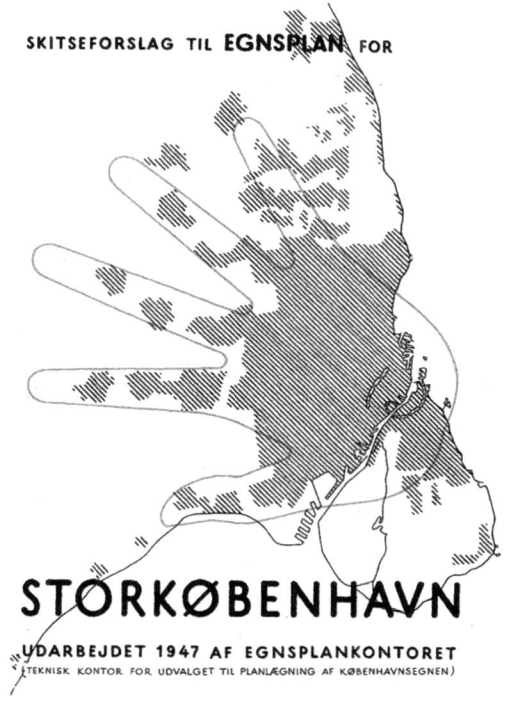

Perhaps most important, metaphors are drawn upon when a factual, down-to-earth term is missing, when both author(s) and reader(s) are called upon to take a flight of imagination in order to make sense of what is being described. Metaphors are the language of uncertainty, and coincide with the coining of new meanings. Metaphors also matter in terms of playfulness of a text: they are about keeping the reader interested and invested in a story welltold. A metaphor such as that of the Sixth Borough is not only persuasive in evoking causalities, but also functions by organizing the sympathies of the reader towards particular perspectives within the narrative. In the example from *Vision 2020*, the metaphor of the Sixth Borough invites New Yorkers to align their own popular knowledge of the city with the view of the policy document. It is important to note that particular metaphors in planning can become so common that citizens and planners alike develop a blind spot to the fact that they are metaphors, in other words, that they are imaginative formulations rather than accurate descriptions of the real world. An example in everyday speech is that of the four "legs" of a table. In planning, an example could be the post-war "finger plan" of Copenhagen (see fig. 6), a plan envisioning development of the Danish capital along five finger-like corridors, which has remained remarkably influential.[35]

4. Applications

Metaphors are powerful rhetorical strategies to situate a plan and a development area as part of recognizable plots. Often, metaphors can be used to legitimize particular courses of action by suggesting a natural or causal relationship by comparison with the natural world or the popular imagination. If a coastal city is described as "under threat" or "under siege" of rising waters, the construction of massive sea walls would seem a logical reaction to the militarization of relationships with the environment. A metaphor such as the "Sixth Borough" gestures towards softer approaches of cohabitation between the city and the water.

Used clumsily or when unconvincing, imaginative metaphors can draw ridicule. Complex or unusual metaphors can also alienate or confuse readers. For planners aiming to draw on the strengths of metaphor in communicating complex problems and their possible solutions, several things are important to bear in mind: 1. At the very least, metaphor is about playfulness and harnessing the imaginative possibilities of language in communicative situations. Using metaphors may catch the readers' imagination and can be an effective way to communicate key points in a memorable way. But ill-advised or unconvincing metaphors in planning will be just as memorable, and may become a rallying point for opposition. 2. Established metaphors are most recognisable and will resonate most easily with the broad population. But they may feel generic and may come with a complex baggage of associated and often suspect meanings – the city as body is one example. 3. Metaphors from local or historical contexts may have the best chance to resonate with local communities. A survey of local narrative features may help to identify metaphors relevant to local communities or stakeholders. As always, narrative used unconvincingly, out of context or in self-contradictory ways runs the risk of backfiring.

Related entries: Emplotment, Genre, Scripts

Further Reading

Ameel, Lieven. "Metaphorizations of the Waterfront in New York City's Comprehensive Waterfront Development Plan *Vision 2020* and Foer's 'The Sixth Borough.'" *Critique: Studies in Contemporary Fiction* 60, no. 3 (2019): 251–62.

Cresswell, Tim. "Weeds, Plagues, and Bodily Secretions: A Geographical Interpretation of Metaphors of Displacement." *Annals of the Association of American Geographers* 87, no. 2 (1997): 330–345.

Donoghue, Denis. *Metaphor*. Cambridge, MA: Harvard University Press, 2014.

Pakarinen, Terttu. *Metaphors in Urban Planning: From Garden City to Zwischenstadt and Netzstadt*. Tampere: Tampere University of Technology, 2010.

Model

1. Definition

A model in the broadest sense of the term is an example worthy of imitation and emulation. More specifically, it is a structural design or blueprint that can be adapted to a variety of purposes. In planning history and theory, a model is also a systematic collocation of data, layered information and inferences which is used to describe and assess a spatial setting and its developmental dynamics.

2. Example

A map of a city with colour-coding in green, yellow or red to represent high, medium or low average incomes per district (see fig. 7) is a model of that city in that it (1) represents the city, (2) does so in highly selective, simplified, abstracted and aggregate form, and (3) does so for specific purposes – possibly to support decisions about where to develop technology parks, plan new housing or community gardening projects or launch social cohesion programmes – while it would be largely useless for other purposes. A model such as an income map offers three services to its readers: (a) it reduces and codes reality, (b) it translates complex settings into readable and reproduceable spatial representations, and (c) it has narrativity, suggesting particular storylines, while discouraging others. Most prominently here, the color-coding suggests a story of an affluent green south and an inner city in economic crisis mode.

Fig. 7: A map of the city of Essen showing average incomes per district.

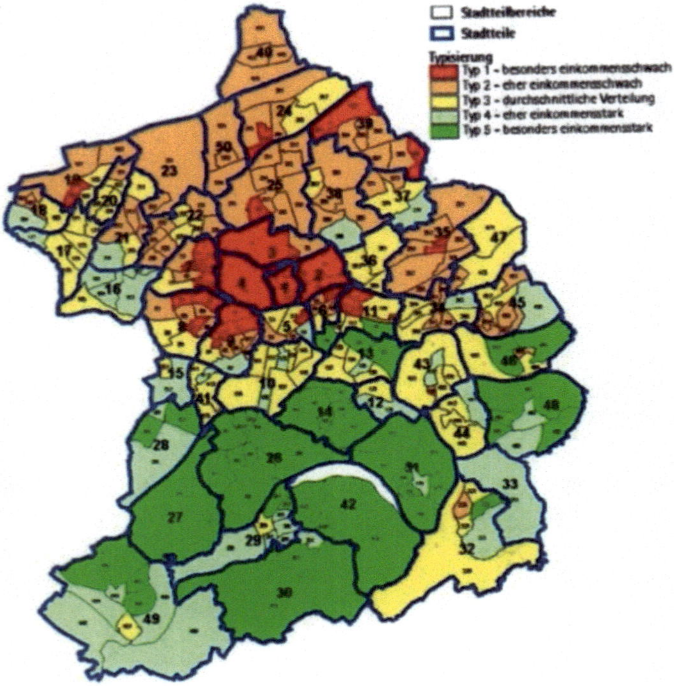

Source: Stadt Essen

3. Explanation

Models offer a simplified physical, digital or mental representation of a more complex outside entity to which they must be functionally or structurally similar in order to successfully serve as a model. Models are devised or chosen for a specific purpose and – depending on that purpose – will selectively focus on different characteristics, elements, connections of the system perceived as central to the specific purpose while ignoring or leaving out others. All models, according to a general theory of models[36], in addition to the three characteristics of being (1) representational, (2) reductive and (3) pragmatic, are characterized by the dual nature of simultaneously being models "of something" and models "for something", since they both reflect and at the same time anticipate what they mean to depict, render understandable and prepare for intervention.[37] Models are *descriptive* renderings of an entity *of* which they are a model and they are – at least implicitly – *prescriptive* blueprints for the design or transformation of a future entity *for* which they are a model. In this respect models resemble narratives: they do not only reflect back upon an existing reality, but actively shape the way the world is perceived and how we see possibilities for change and development.

In urban modelling, the key methodological challenge has been the successful combination of quantitative and qualitative models and the effort to complement the strengths of each to minimize the respective limitations of either type of model. Douglass B. Lee famously listed the seven "sins" of models in his "Requiem for Large-scale Urban Models" (1973), a trenchant critique of the adaptation of quantitative computational models that had originally been devised for space and military operations to urban planning problems. Models can be too comprehensive, too gross, data consuming, structurally inert, complex, mechanical and expensive, according to Lee.[38] Quantitative models – designed as decision support tools, for instance – are characterized by quantification, abstraction from individuality and specificity and by aggregation and thus are frequently not concerned with local or individual characteristics. Qualitative models are frequently designed to do just that: to represent local or individual specificity. Literary texts can be seen as a particular type of qualitative model in that they focus precisely on the representation of specific places, of individual responses and patterns of sense-making. In their selection of which elements of complex urban reality to incorporate and what to leave out and in their inventive license, literary texts are virtually diametrically opposed to quantitative models seeking data driven abstraction, scaling and applicability to a wide range of settings. But these distinctive types of models shape each other in multiple ways, since empirical data and preconceived principles shape qualitative as well as quantitative analyses and scenario building.

Literary texts as qualitative forms of 'modelling' urban complexity enable views of planning problems that acknowledge the possibility of disruption and invention as much as the possibility of backsliding and inversion. Additionally, they can serve as exemplary models that inspire emulation, thus allowing for slow transformations of the reality depicted in the model.

4. Applications

Qualitative models established in literary texts capture place-specificity, uniqueness and individuality and it is little surprising that they are frequently employed in narrative mapping exercises that accompany concrete urban planning activities. These qualitative models occasionally contradict quantitative models that abstract from the individual, and the specific to arrive at more generally valid conclusions or predictions. As increasingly frequent collaboration between planning experts and science fiction writers shows, literary texts as models *of* and models *for* urban realities also have a crucial role to play in developing scenarios. Thus, the German Federal Institute for Building, Urban and Spatial Research (BBSR) recently issued a study entitled *Learning from Science Fiction Cities* that discussed potential uses to be made of the extent to which literature, but also film and video games, contain modelling elements that address questions of urban governance, infrastructure and the built environment.[39] Planning for uncertainty initiatives have increasingly adopted "what if" scenario building and gaming in order to learn from models of urban development developed in literature and popular culture.

Related entries: Narrative, Scenario, Scripts, Travelling Models

Further Reading

Gurr, Jens Martin. *Charting Literary Urban Studies: Texts as Models of and for the City*. New York, London: Routledge, 2021.

te Brömmelstroet, Marco, Peter Pelzer, Stan Geertman. "Forty Years after Lee's Requiem: Are We Beyond the Seven Sins?" *Environment and Planning. B, Planning & Design* 41, no. 3 (2014): 381–387.

Batty, Michael. "Chapter 9: Urban Simulation." *The New Science of Cities*. Boston: MIT Press, 2013. 271–299.

Narrative

1. Definition

Narrative is when somebody at a particular occasion tells somebody else a real or fictional story.[40] An example of a narrative is someone telling someone else a personal anecdote; or when the narrator in a literary novel recounts a story to the reader; or when a newspaper reporter breaks a news story. This broad definition of narrative can be applied with relative ease to urban planning documents: planners (or a planning agency) can be seen as the narrator(s) who recount a *story*, usually aimed at the inhabitants of the area affected by planning, at the stakeholders, or at future planners. Most of the recounted events will be real enough (rather than fictional), but planning documents also tend to involve elements that are not real (yet), such as claims about what an area will look and feel like in the future.

To fully define a narrative, it is necessary to also define what makes a story. A story is defined here as having: 1. clearly outlined human (or human-like) characters doing things; 2. a change of situation, typically (but not necessarily) from balance to imbalance to balance; and 3. an association with mental states: human desires, fears, hopes may drive the events in the story, which are relevant also for why we are interested to hear about a particular story.[41]

2. Example

When the Helsinki mayor Jussi Pajunen spoke to reporters in September 2008, on the verge of the biggest boom in waterfront development in the Finnish capital in over a century, he told his audience, drawing on the age-old image of Helsinki as feminine figure:

> "The daughter of the Baltic [Helsinki] is submitting herself to the sea, her former hunting grounds."[42]

Fig. 8: Havis Amanda, allegory of Helsinki as daughter of the Baltic.

Source: https://commons.wikimedia.org/wiki/File:Havis_Amanda_sculpture_by_Ville_Vallgren_in_Helsinki_(29484842696).jpg. Archives of the Finnish Broadcasting Company Yle

Here we have someone (Pajunen) telling someone (reporters, and through them, the general public) on some occasion (September 2008) that something happened (Helsinki's development is opening up toward the shore and reaching into the sea) for a particular reason, and drawing on particular symbolic imagery to provide a sense of historical continuity and causality to the story he tells (see fig. 8).

We here see something quite typical of how narratives in the context of planning tend to be presented: the city itself appears as the human (or human-like) main character in the story Pajunen tells, and a change for the better is at the heart of the story.

3. Explanation

Planning has been defined also as a form of "persuasive storytelling".[43] The focus on persuasiveness suggests that planning narratives are primarily about convincing the intended audiences about the course of action to be taken, and using rhetorical strategies to reach their goal. The speech by Mayor Pajunen used rhetorics – the symbol of the daughter of the Baltic Sea – to present unprecedented urban development as in line with the historical image of the Finnish capital, even as rectifying a historical wrong. Several of the narratives found in contemporary planning documents issued by the Helsinki City Planning Department use similar rhetorical images.

But narrative also involves other elements. Narratives are means of making sense of the world, and contain frames of knowledge that describe reality but also prescribe how we are able to make sense of reality, and how we are able to envision our possibilities to change the world. Storytelling in this sense provides "a major reservoir of the cultural baggage that enables us to make meaning out of a chaotic world and the incomprehensible events taking place in it".[44] When planners engage in storytelling, they are not only persuading audiences, but also trying to make sense of the world. And narrative tends to include a sense of entertainment, of enjoyment in the creative performativity of storytelling, even in the bleakest of stories. Bringing out the narrative elements in planning may be a more effective mode of communicating not only because it draws on pervasive rhetorical strategies, but also because it speaks to the human interest of being gripped by a compelling story in its own right.

There are a wide variety of different kinds of narratives in the context of urban planning. People tell each other personal stories of a city that changes; policy makers and politicians tell the media stories of decisions for a brighter future; stories are written down in letters or posted on social media. Urban planning itself is also a form of storytelling, in which planners communicate with other branches in the city, stakeholders and private interests through documents, meetings, and media outreach.

In terms of how narratives relate to urban planning, three different categories can be outlined:

1. The existing narratives of a location, prior to planning: local, everyday stories; artistic representations; historical or other documents;
2. The narrative texts and practices involved in planning itself;
3. The narratives parallel or posterior to the planning proper, for example in branding or placemaking strategies, but also in the way local stories react to and communicate with planning and development of an area.

These three types are called here, respectively: narratives *for* planning (narratives that planners can draw on in their practices); narratives *in* planning (the planning process as a form of story-telling); narratives *of* planning (the storytelling that follows in the wake of planning practices).

4. Applications

Narratives *for* planning are perhaps what has interested planners most during the past few decades: the experiential local knowledge embedded in local narratives, from oral histories to literary novels to songs and folklore about a particular place. The cartography of narratives of place has been advocated by several urban thinkers as a method to enable planners to form an idea of the broader narrative framework within which they are operating. A narrative mapping of a particular area, guided by conceptualizations from literary and narrative theory, would approach narratives not in the way these describe (rather statically) a particular environment as mere dots on a map. It would, instead, focus on the dynamic role played by location in relation to plot and character development; on metaphorizations of the area, and on the interaction between the location and the literary frames or genre features it triggers.

Narratives *for* planning are increasingly seen as important experiential information whose successful adaptation in the planning process could lead to more inclusive and democratic planning. However, if the aim of participatory narrative practices is to let local voices be heard more clearly, efforts should be made to ensure a transparent selection process and a coherent analysis and adaptation of these narratives. To ensure that the original narratives do not get lost in the process of summarizing and re-writing, one first step would be to at least keep these available for future reference, for example in the form of open-access databases.

Related entries: Future Narratives, Narrativity, Scenario

Further Reading

Ameel, Lieven. "Towards a Narrative Typology of Urban Planning Narratives for, in, and of Planning in Jätkäsaari, Helsinki." *Urban Design International* 22, no. 4 (2016): 318–330.

Herman, David. *Basic Elements of Narrative*. Oxford: Wiley-Blackwell, 2009.

Ryan, Marie-Laure. *A New Anatomy of Storyworlds. What Is, What If, As If.* Columbus: Ohio State University Press, 2022.

Throgmorton, James A. "Storytelling and City Crafting in a Contested Age: One Mayor's Practice Story." *Planners in Politics: Do They Make a Difference?* Ed. Louis Albrechts. Cheltenham, UK: Edward Elgar Publications, 2020. 174–197.

Narrativity

1. Definition

Narrativity is the ability to evoke stories.[45] A building, or a built environment, cannot literally tell a story, neither can a map or a random list. But buildings, maps, and urban form can have narrativity, by suggesting or bringing to mind particular stories.

2. Example

An image in a planning document that shows what a future seashore development will look like, such as the view of Hanseatic-looking future buildings at the West Harbor's waterfront in Helsinki (see fig. 9), can be deeply suggestive of past and future stories of the area and its development. In this particular case, the image is evocative of a story that feeds into the overall narrative of planning of the Helsinki waterfront in terms of integration of the waterfront within the existing urban structure. The image gestures toward historical continuation and highlights the moment of completion towards which the plan is moving. Similar to an image, a building or construction, too, can have narrativity, something which the Helsinki planning department implicitly suggests in the document "Maritime Helsinki in the City Plan", which describes possible windmill farms on the Helsinki coast as communicating to the future viewer a message that evokes the story of "a city of high-tech and ecological know-how", where "sustainable energy should be visible".[46]

Fig. 9: Waterfront in the West Harbour of Helsinki.

© Lundgaard & Tranberg Arkitekter

3. Explanation

Narrativity is one way in which urban development can be linked to an area's existing history or to a community's heritage. Planning with narrativity is also a way to evoke place identities where stories of an area's identity are only gradually taking shape, such as in a post-industrial harbour development or a new suburban development. Much of what has fallen under the term of "placemaking" in planning deals in effect with designing with narativity. Red bricks and industrial rail lines that are kept as part of a new development may be intended to activate the narrativity of such historical built elements, and to evoke stories of the working-class history of an area. Artworks in public space can have a similar aim. The work "Line Drawn in the Water", an artwork twelve meters high in the East Harbour development in Helsinki, consists of a canoe raised on a curved metal pole, which references historical and contemporary sea-faring technologies as well as the area's maritime history.

Place name practices are one way in which planners, in collaboration with naming agencies, engage with the narrativity of the built environment. The Helsinki East Harbour showcases several examples of imaginative use of place names: names of streets and public squares or quays refer evocatively to the area's blue-collar history, to its maritime history, or to ships that had their home port in the area, as well as to the islands erased in the construction of the harbour during the twentieth century.

Working with narrativity may also be about creating a space for specific kinds of activities with the aim to give rise to new stories of how a particular area is used. This comes close to what Richard Sennett had in mind when calling for "narrative spaces"; spaces that "permit certain properties of narratives to operate in everyday life."[47] In the planning of the Jätkäsaari area in Helsinki, elevation differences in the central park were explicitly designed to invite sledging activities. Planning for temporary use is one other way in which an area's narrativity can be steered in particular directions. In the Helsinki East Harbour, various examples of temporary use, including a DIY sauna and what is advertised as the longest graffiti wall in Northern Europe, feed into broader narratives of the area as a creative hub.[48]

4. Applications

When aiming to enhance or steer the narrativity of the built environment, it makes sense to aim for storylines that are aligned with (or at the very least aware of) the historical background of the area, that are coherent with the overall narratives in the planning area, and that have a reasonable degree of probability. Here, as elsewhere, it may be good to bear in mind Aristotle's suggestion to storytellers to focus on events that are "possible by the standards of probability and necessity".[49] Planners and policy makers will be taken to task when the stories that are evoked by plans, 3D images, naming practices, and buildings, are one-sided, incoherent, improbable, or when they are lacking in inclusiveness and diversity. Signs in the public realm are one way in which the narrativity of an area can be geared toward an otherwise lost or silenced history, from memorial plaques with references to disappearing natural diversity, to stumbling stones

(*Stolpersteine*) commemorating the latest place of residence of victims of Nazi extermination or persecution, in Germany and elsewhere. Period and genre conventions will define in part how the narrativity of a built environment evokes new stories. A medieval castle in the city may have been meant in its original context to evoke stories about the power of a feudal lord over recalcitrant burgers, but in the twenty-first century, its meanings will have dramatically shifted. Red bricks in twenty-first century developments may have been intended to suggest working-class history, but may be interpreted by onlookers as yet another example of generic planning, or as an inability on the planners' side to think beyond established clichés of a particular city. Construction of the story itself happens in the head of the onlooker, and as always, there is the possibility of unintended meanings and associations. If interventions in public space, or new building developments, are constructed with little concern for past layers of meaning, or for future users or inhabitants, these will find means to circumvent intended use or meaning. The challenge of planning with narrativity is to provide a measure of coherence while also being aware of the multiplicity and open-endedness of how city narratives are used and read.

Related entries: Closure, Genre, Narrative, Palimpsest, Path-dependency

Further Reading

Ameel, Lieven. *The Narrative Turn in Urban Planning: Plotting the Helsinki Waterfront*. New York: Routledge, 2021.

Borosch, Juliane, Barbara Buchenau. "Walking Down Woodward – (Re-)Telling a City's Stories through Urban Figures." *City Scripts: Narratives of Postindustrial Urban Futures*. Ed. Barbara Buchenau, Jens Martin Gurr, Maria Sulimma. Columbus: Ohio State University Press, forthcoming.

Ryan, Marie-Laure. "The Modes of Narrativity and their Visual Metaphors." *Style* 26, no. 3 (1992): 368–387.

White, Hayden. "The Value of Narrativity in the Representation of Reality." *On Narrative*. Ed. W.J.T. Mitchell. Chicago: University of Chicago Press, 1981. 1–24.

Palimpsest

1. Definition

Originally, a palimpsest is a paper or parchment which, in times when writing material was scarce, was written on more than once, with a first layer of writing being written over in such a way that older layers are still (partly) legible underneath (see fig. 10). Given the multiple historical layers still more or less visible in many present-day cities, these are often suggestively described in terms of the palimpsest.

Fig. 10: *The Archimedes Palimpsest.*

Source: http://archimedespalimpsest.org/

2. Example

Many contemporary European cities can be regarded as palimpsests in built form: This is true of the city of Essen in Germany's Ruhr region, for instance, in which an underlying medieval layout is still visible in the kidney-shaped form of the inner city and in the course of present-day roads around the city center. Similarly, the palimpsest may be regarded as a suggestive concept to describe the location and shape of streets which still trace a winding way in between buildings long gone, or the presence of churches from centuries ago, churches that might each in turn be seen as palimpsests if they have gone through various phases of enlargement, redesign and modernization.

3. Explanation

The city is a space in which different historical periods are preserved in different layers of the urban fabric, which in turn preserve the memory of previous epochs associated with the built environment. The city can thus be seen as a spatialized form of urban memory materialized in palimpsestic structures. In addition to the built environment, local urban memory, too, can be understood as palimpsestic: Particular neighbourhoods may be characterized by a dense layering of memories, anecdotes, urban legends triggered by established festivities, parades or specific buildings such as long-existing pubs or restaurants, which may be associated with legendary local figures formally or informally memorialized in street names, memorial plaques or drinking songs, poems, or nicknames. Urban sociologist Gerald D. Suttles has introduced the notion of "the cumulative texture of local urban culture" to describe this phenomonen. The layering of immaterial urban memory can also be conceptualized as a palimpsest. In his vastly influential *Arcades Project* (*Das Passagenwerk*, 1927–1940), a 1000-page experimental work on the 19th-century arcades in Paris, which proceeds largely through the juxtaposition of some 3500 quotations from 800 different sources, German philosopher Walter Benjamin developed the related notion of "superposition"⁵⁰. This is Benjamin's term for the interpenetration of different layers of time in urban space. Given a certain frame of mind, this simultaneous co-presence of different historical layers can be perceived and understood by an urban observer. Benjamin clearly characterizes this frame of mind as that of the flâneur, the disinterested observer of city life who walks the city without an agenda: "Thanks to this phenomenon, anything that ever potentially happened in a space is perceived simultaneously. Space winks at the flâneur: 'Well, whatever may have happened here?'".⁵¹ Thus, superposition refers to both the temporal layering and to the ability to perceive it. This view allows one to conceptualize the importance of an observer's knowledge of a site's previous history even if there are no visible traces left, while the notion of the palimpsest suggests that older layers are still visible.

For the urban planner and for anyone trying to understand the historical fabric of the city, superposition can also refer to a conscious approach or even technique. The ability to perceive how an ensemble of modern buildings fits into its historical contexts in terms of the remaining elements of past historical periods, but also in the way it may even cite a pre-war building that might have stood on the same plot – and thus the ability to perceive the continuing presence of the past in the palimpsestic layering of the built environment – is crucial for any planning effort in the same environment.⁵²

4. Applications

The notion of the city as a palimpsest and as a spatialized form of memory in which physical layers of the built environment call to mind immaterial layers of urban memory is highly relevant to the concept of "careful urban renewal" ("behutsame Stadterneuerung"), which, not least through processes of international development cooperation, has spread from Europe to many places in both the Global North and the Global South. Numerous projects in China, for instance, try to maintain the historical urban fabric and external appearance of buildings while technically and functionally retrofitting them for adaptive re-use with the intention of preserving historical layers of the city. While most strongly associated with European cities, the notion of the palimpsest has long also been used for cities globally, occasionally with a shift in emphasis away from the preservation and legibility of older layers towards their erasure, in the case of excavation or the demolition of later additions to make visible earlier material layers, or when entire neighborhoods are razed to make way for new development.[53]

Related entries: Metaphor, Polyphony

Further Reading

Dillon, Sarah. *The Palimpsest: Literature, Criticism, Theory*. New York: Continuum, 2007.

Gurr, Jens Martin. "Reversing Perspectives: Urban Memory in Built and Literary Post-Industrial Cities." Gurr. *Charting Literary Urban Studies: Texts as Models of and for the City*. New York: Routledge, 2021. 84–109. Link to open access version: https://doi.org/10.4324/9781003111009.

Gurr, Jens Martin. "Palimpsest." *The Routledge Companion to Literary Urban Studies*. Ed. Lieven Ameel. New York/London: Routledge, 2022. 72–86.

Suttles, Gerald D. "The Cumulative Texture of Local Urban Culture." *American Journal of Sociology* 90, no. 2 (1984): 283–304.

Path-dependency

1. Definition

Path-dependencies are defined as developments in which a situation or decision predetermines future development; present-day decisions might thus limit the range of options for future decision makers.

2. Example

Big infrastructural works for mobility or energy production provide the clearest contemporary examples of decisions that create path-dependency. The building of a nuclear power station creates a legacy not only of dangerous nuclear waste that will need to be safely stored for thousands of years, it also predetermines social processes and power relations. The specific risks associated with the management of a nuclear power station in critical situations may require rapid expert intervention and quick decision-making that bypass democratic decision-making processes. The decision to build a nuclear power station can thus be said to create multiple – technological, environmental, social and political – path-dependencies.[54]

Cities located at the water are particularly vulnerable to decisions that create path-dependencies. Bridge heights, for instance, will limit the scale of vessels that can pass under them; the entry points and size of tunnels can define ingoing and outgoing traffic, and everything that builds up in connection with such traffic, for generations.

A literal example of path-dependency can be seen in the development phases of the Kajaani Castle in Finland, one of the northernmost medieval castles in the world. The castle developed on the location of an island in the Kajaani river, with a bridge connecting both riverbanks and the island. Gradually, the surroundings of the castle saw the development of a small city, split in two by the river. Technological advances in the twentieth century meant that a modern bridge connecting both parts of the city could easily have been built in other locations than the one provided by the island crossing. The modern bridge and motorway from 1937, however, closely follow the late medieval path, cutting through the historical fortress (see figs. 11 a/b).

Fig. 11a: Kajaani Castle in a drawing from 1729. Krigsarkivet, Stockholm.

Fig. 11b: Ruins of Kajaani Castle with modern bridge (built in 1937).

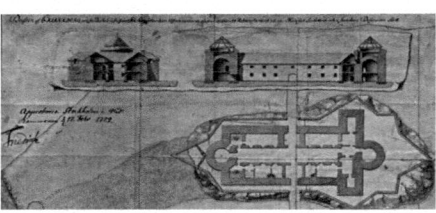

Source: https://commons.wikimedia.org/wiki/File:Cajanaborg.jpg

Image by Henrik Jansson

3. Explanation

If one assumes that the built environment shapes social processes just as social processes shape the built environment[55], it is clear that planning decisions – especially if they are decisions which either create long-term structures or which generate technological lock-ins – have long-term consequences for the living conditions in cities. Just as decisions for technological standards in markets with a need for a systemic fit of different components create technological lock-in (think DOS vs. Mac or the printer market), planning decisions create path-dependencies which impose on future generations the consequences of blind spots or short-sightedness at the time of making the decision. A case in point is the decision in cities worldwide in the 20th century to plan cities around individual automotive mobility at a time when environmental degradation, climate change, or geopolitical considerations with regard to fossil fuel dependencies were not an active issue. This created path dependencies in terms of functional zoning, the use of space, (dis-)incentives for living in the city or in suburbs, environmental developments, urban public health and a range of other fields. A crucial issue for contemporary planning is the question what future generations will recognize as present-day blind spots, limitations or unquestioned pre-occupations and which path-dependencies they will have led to.

Insights into the limitations of planning in recent decades have further highlighted the need to consider path-dependencies in urban planning: this is true both for insights into the role of emergence – spontaneous, unplanned (and unplannable) processes in urban development – as well as for the more general insight into the limits of planning and into the constraints of planning in and for conditions of uncertainty.

From the perspective of literary and narrative studies, path-dependency is bound up with the way in which beginnings set the stage for particular storytelling patterns to develop. The way a particular plot is set out in the beginning of a narrative – including planning narratives – can be called "inaugural emplotment": the almost prophetic, suggestive, and forward-looking manner of positioning a particular spatial setting within narrative developments that take on an aspect of inevitability.[56] Specific modes of emplotment – for instance comedy, tragedy, satire, or romance[57] – with their generic implications as well as central tropes and references to established patterns of narrative sense-making – can be said to suggest or even determine specific path dependencies, outcomes, inclusions and exclusions. Plans that emplot the development of a neighbourhood in explicitly stated terms of 'realizing its potential', 'finding a voice', 'coming to be integrated into the city', for example, can be linked to the genre of the *Bildungsroman*.

4. Applications

Just as certain plot patterns can create a type of narrative path dependency by strongly suggesting specific outcomes, some metaphors – often unintentionally or even against the most likely intended logic of a planning text – can suggest narrative patterns, again with associated outcomes, inclusions and exclusions. For instance, the common notion of specific groups – artists, students, members of the LGBTQ community – as so-called pioneers on the frontier of urban revitalization, can be shown to actualize the implications of the frontier trope by raising the question who the ostensible 'hostile native Americans' implied in this trope might be, suggesting potentially divisive and agonistic patterns in urban development as well as patterns of inclusion and exclusion. Research on such patterns relies on recent developments in cognitive science and their repercussions in literary and cultural studies, which have foregrounded the power of figurative thought and the way in which cognitive models guiding thought and behaviour rely on figures of speech and thought. In attempts at securing socially integrative planning, attention to the implications of the chosen metaphor or narrative patterns and their suggested path-dependencies can be vital to detecting and avoiding unintended or counter-intuitive suggestions.

More generally, insights into the role of path-dependencies for planning and insights into the limits of planning have contributed to what might be referred to as a new modesty in planning after the perceived failure of many high-flying plans in 20th-century planning (for instance, large-scale modernist planning in the wake of Le Corbusier). This more modest type of planning seeks to limit path-dependencies by allowing for reversible planning decisions. The city of Portland, Oregon, has often been credited with pioneering such planning principles in the early 2000s.[58]

Similar to our remarks in the context of "Closure", where we suggested the possibility of more open endings in planning narratives, it would be beneficial to think of narrative beginnings – and the metaphors and modes of emplotment planners use in beginnings – in planning and policy in terms of possible path-dependency, with the aim of retaining an openness for multiple pathways.

Related entries: Closure, Emplotment, Genre, Scenario, Scripts

Further Reading

Gurr, Jens Martin. "Narrative Path Dependencies: From Scenario Building in Literary Texts to the Narratology and Rhetoric of Pragmatic Texts." Gurr. *Charting Literary Urban Studies: Texts as Models of and for the City*. New York: Routledge, 2021. 125–140 [open access, https://doi.org/10.4324/9781003111009].

Hein, Carola, Dirk Schubert. "Resilience and Path Dependence: A Comparative Study of the Port Cities of London, Hamburg, and Philadelphia." *Journal of Urban History* 47, no. 2 (2021): 389–419.

Pierson, Paul. "Increasing Returns, Path Dependence, and the Study of Politics." *The American Political Science Review* 94, no. 2 (2000): 251–267.

Placemaking

1. Definition

Placemaking may be defined as the art of creating recognizable, unique and liveable places with a distinct place identity, an identity that works both internally, to residents and users of a place, and externally, to people outside, who may not even have visited the place in question but who nonetheless have an image or mental map of that place. While placemaking has a lot to do with iconic buildings, attractive green spaces and livability, it relies heavily on narratives, performances and medial images.

2. Example

Juliane Borosch discusses a striking example of a collective placemaking that is both community- and corporation-driven.[59] It has been unfolding in Detroit since the early 2020s. Here, urban planners, citizens, artists and a global corporation are not explicitly working together, but each of these pivotal actors in urban development plays a critical role in a major push to change iconic parts of the urban infrastructure. The goal is placemaking by "changing the metonymy".[60] This means that there is a concerted effort to change the fact that Detroit has come to stand for global postindustrial decline and socio-economic disintegration, while vacant iconic buildings in Detroit have come to stand for the loss of urban jobs and urban functions. Rather than destroying this metonymic relationship by, for instance, implementing new urban infrastructure, participants from a variety of social sectors have reassessed the meaning of iconic buildings that had lost their former infrastructural purpose. And they are redefining these buildings as both sites of heritage and future ambitions. In this architectural case of placemaking, a single building such as Michigan Central Station (see fig. 12), beginning with its inception through its heyday and its decline as much as its revitalization, is understood and accepted "as the face that Detroit would [...] show to the world."[61] After the Ford Motor Company bought the disintegrating Michigan Central Station in order to turn it into the hub of its "new mobility campus", it grounded its repurposing plans in the history of popular uses of the building as both a "screen" on which to literally project the future of the city (by multimedial projections onto the façade, which also allowed participants to "broadcast" their individual hopes for Detroit to Detroit audiences) and as a "second face" through which to read the city.[62] Ford's conversion of the building into what the central virtual exhibit is currently calling "the epicenter of innovation at the intersection of technology and society" indicates the importance of placemaking practices for big businesses as much as for city dwellers and administrations.[63]

Fig. 12: Michigan Central Station under Reconstruction, courtesy of Juliane Borosch

3. Explanation

Research on placemaking – particularly on place perception and mental maps – informed by environmental psychology argues that "[p]erceptions of places (are) derived from people's information flow, such as newspapers, magazines, books, movies, television, and other forms of the media".[64] For virtually all places about which we have at least some information – accurate or not –, even first-hand personal experience is pre-formed by images and stories about that place. This obviously has profound consequences for tourism, investment decisions or decisions about where to take a place of residence, because hardly a place people choose to relocate to, search for a job or spend their holidays will be a clean slate to them before they first see it for themselves. While this phenomenon is highlighted by the 'instagrammification' of tourist destinations with, for instance, the deliberate creation of photo opportunities, the phenomenon is much older than social media.

In spatial research, there is a common distinction between space – often understood as abstract, non-personalized and devoid of a specific identity – and place – a space that, not least through stories, memories, anecdotes and personal associations, has become meaningful to an individual or a group. This means that one person's abstract space can at the same time be another person's meaningful place. A classic account of places commonly perceived as lacking meaning and specificity is anthropologist Marc Augé's *Non-Places: An Introduction to Supermodernity*, which describes places like airports, shopping-malls, train stations or chain hotels as classic examples of non-places. It is clear, however, that such an anonymous place can become a highly specific, meaningful place to an individual if it becomes associated with personal experiences and stories.

As for the identity and specificity of individual cities, German sociologists Helmuth Berking and Martina Löw introduced the notion of an "intrinsic logic of cities".[65] Their notion implies that the identity and historical development of a city (and, by implication, of a site, a neighborhood or an entire region) needs to be taken into account when attempting to understand its present or to shape its future development. This also suggests that the stories crafted to promote a city or a region should carefully be made to suit an audience's expectations or assumptions: a story does not need to confirm such preconceptions but at least needs to be aware of them and should plausibly engage with them.

4. Applications

Should a post-industrial city use a long-defunct iconic building or its manufacturing, coal and steel past in its self-promotion? This will be emotionally charged and meaningful to many residents, but to overly rely on it runs the risk of musealisation and of being perceived as remaining stuck in the past. In their placemaking activities, such cities will therefore frequently seek to combine references to their past with something that is decidedly oriented toward the future, such as new types of mobility and energy production.

In a 2018 image film, for instance, the regional economic development agency of Germany's Ruhr region sought to promote it as a vibrant and attractive region to live, work and invest in.[66] Accompanied by appropriate imagery, a voice-over narrator highlighted the comparatively low cost of living, the fairly relaxed housing market, the large number of students in the region, and its diverse population. A section on the region's vibrant cultural and night life had the narrator say "We are the city that never sleeps – sorry, New York". While surely meant to be understood as a provocative, jocular remark, the phrase can also be read as displaying a problematic uncertainty about one's own position. "Know what league you're boxing in!" is how a group of students from the Ruhr region responded to this video in a placemaking seminar. In this case, the language used to promote a place is clearly at odds with an audience's perception of what is realistic – or at least attainable. Moreover, the over-emphasis on authoritative storytelling in this clip indicates a detrimental faith in cinematic place-making at the expense of concrete efforts to engage communities, enhance livability, foster a visual identity or develop compelling and differentiated urban development strategies.

A further point to bear in mind is the need to distinguish internal from external audiences of place-making: While there may be targeted messaging that works for both audiences, there may also be messages more suitable to making residents feel at home in a region than to addressing external potential visitors or investors – and vice versa.

Finally, while the importance of narratives to placemaking has been increasingly recognized (they can clearly be central to endowing a place with meaning and to promoting place identity and specificity), it also seems appropriate to warn against *over*-emphasizing the power of stories: while narrative strategies and strategic narratives are vital to urban development, they should not be expected to be able to *replace* compelling and differentiated urban development strategies. Placemaking, it is clear, is a complex undertaking that has to be driven by dedicated communities, attentive urban administrators and businesses or corporations that have a credible local engagement. This endeavor needs to confront successes as much as failures in order to take long-lasting effect.[67]

Related entries: Narrative, Path-dependency, Scenario, Scripts

Further Reading

Buchenau, Barbara, Jens Martin Gurr, Maria Sulimma, eds. *City Scripts: Narratives of Postindustrial Urban Futures*. Columbus: Ohio State University Press, forthcoming.

Courage, Cara, Tom Borrup, Maria Rosario Jackson, Kylie Legge, Anita McKeown, Louise Platt, Jason Schupbach, eds. *The Routledge Handbook of Placemaking*. London/New York: Routledge, 2021.

Jacobs, Jane. *The Death and Life of Great American Cities*. New York: Random House, 1961.

Loh, Carolyn G. et al. "Placemaking in Practice: Municipal Arts and Cultural Plans' Approaches to Placemaking and Creative Placemaking." *Journal of Planning Education and Research* (2022): n. pag. https://doi.org/10.1177/0739456X221100503.

Polyphony

1. Definition

Polyphony is literally multi-voicedness: the ability of a text or story to include several different voices and perspectives, undisrupted by an overarching authorial voice.

2. Example

Located in Antwerp along the river Scheldt, the flood wall of the river quays displays an ingenious piece of poetry in public space: the Quay Poem, composed by the official Antwerp city poet Peter Holvoet-Hanssen (see fig. 13). The poem was painted in 2011 in bright white on more than 3 kilometres of length of the concrete wall looking out to the river Scheldt. The text is a collage of different voices: more than 500 inhabitants of Antwerp sent in verses and lines, on the basis of which the city poet composed what he called a "stream of words of the city".[68] The text also includes selected verses from other Antwerp poets. One particularity of the text is that the different voices are not presented in summarised or paraphrased form, but are explicitly indicated as separate utterances by being placed within quotation marks. As such, the text provides a true multi-voiced narrative of and by the city's inhabitants. The poem was realised in part by the city's planning department as part of their outreach for the redevelopment of the quays. But more than anything, the polyphonic Quay Poem provides a stark contrast with the dominant single-voicedness that is typically found in urban planning texts – including those produced by the city of Antwerp.

Fig. 13: Image of the Antwerp Quay poem.

Photo by Lieven Ameel. 30 April 2019

3. Explanation

Cities are by definition polyphonic; they are always "the intersections of multiple narratives".[69] As planning has become more dialogic and deliberative, it increasingly aims to include a more diverse range of urban voices and to take into account more diverse kinds of knowledge. In other words, it aims to become more *polyphonic*: planning that is aware of, and embraces, the manifold voices it caters for.

A first step is to survey the diversity of different local voices that exist prior to planning, an overview of narratives *for* planning.[70] Several planning thinkers emphasize the plurality of narratives that arises from a closer look at local narratives. Perhaps the biggest challenge encountered is that of enabling planning not just to reflect on the diversity of urban narratives, but to incorporate the local narratives in such a way that "policies and plans … represent a collective authorship between people and planners".[71] One of the principal aims of the 'discursive', 'dialogic' or 'narrative' turn in planning practices was to let the hitherto passive recipients of planning narratives become a more active part of the story-telling in which they are enmeshed, to let the 'objects' of formerly mono-voiced practices be active producers of the meaning-making that affects them.

In literary studies, polyphony is connected first and foremost with the figure of Mikhail Bakhtin (1984), who developed his theory of polyphony in an influential study of the work of Dostoevsky. For the study of urban planning narratives, Bakhtin's concept of polyphony has particular relevance because of the way it examines different voices within one and the same body of text. The inclusion of a multitude of voices, in the terminology of Bakhtin, does not come from outside the text, then, to enrich it, but it is part and parcel of the text itself, within it, and taking the form of a dialogic imagination. The Quay Poem by Holvoet-Hanssen is a unique example of such dialogic imagination at work: a text that gives voice to other authors beyond the one named author, and that continues multiple voices that exist independently. Interestingly, for our purpose, Bakhtin does not define polyphony as merely a literary method, but also as a principle of human relationships.[72]

4. Applications

The polyphony of urban voices touches on some of the most urgent questions faced by planning practices, in particular the legitimacy of planning practices and the status of different kinds of knowledge. With current advances in participatory planning geographic information systems (PPGIS), the mapping of different experiences of a particular planning site has become ever more feasible. But gathering big data on a place through PPGIS is not the same as being able to make sense of the wealth of qualitative data that may be the result. The greatest challenge is not to accurately survey urban polyphony, but to create planning texts that include such a diversity of voices.

Can planning by truly polyphonic? Is it possible for urban planning practices, with their binding legal procedures and their highly formalized textual and visual outcomes, to include diverging voices that are independent of the authorial voice of the planning department? Some incremental polyphonic elements can be be part of a move toward more polyphonic planning. One element is to include, within a planning text, some relevant personal stories, for example as vignettes set apart from the main text. This has become a widespread practice that can also be seen in *Between City and Stream*, the masterplan for the Antwerp Quays. The master plan is announced as "a story that in many respects is told by many"; and readers will hear "the many voices [of 800 participating Antwerp citizens] resounding throughout many places in this brochure." (3)

There is always the risk that such quotes constitute no more than mere tokenism on the ladder of participation.[73] But, especially when quoted in their original form, and with proper information on the context of the original utterance, such diverging voices are able not only to give a sense of the polyphony underlying one particular plan, but to bring in some of that complexity into its storytelling. The typical way of using vignettes of quotes by inhabitants is to use them to support the key arguments within a planning narrative. But Bakhtinian polyphony contains the suggestion that a narrative text may contain contradictory narratives, and this consequence of polyphony is worth considering. Would it be possible to include in a plan the stories – even by way of vignettes – of how different inhabitants see the development of their city, even if these are stories that run counter to the dominant current? We are not aware of planning texts that deliberately set out to do this, but including such a truly polyphonic, even contradictory, set of storylines may have unforeseen benefits. It could point the way towards more inclusive planning, and allow possibilities for multiple alternatives, which may limit the path-dependency of a particular plan.

Related entries: Closure, Path-dependency

Further Reading

Ameel, Lieven. "Narrative Mapping and Polyphony in Urban Planning." *Yhdyskuntasuunnittelu / Finnish Journal for Urban Studies* 2 (2016): 20–40.

Antwerp. *Tussen stad en stroom. Het Masterplan Scheldekaaien Antwerpen*. Antwerp: GSA, 2011.

Bakhtin, Mikhail. *Problems of Dostoevsky's Poetics*. Minneapolis: University of Minnesota Press, 1984.

Finnegan, Ruth. *Tales of the City: A Study of Narrative and Urban Life*. Cambridge: Cambridge University Press, 1998.

Holloway, Julian, James Kneale. "Mikhail Bakhtin: Dialogics of Space." *Thinking Space*. Ed. Mike Crang, Nigel Thrift. London: Routledge, 2000. 71–88.

Sandercock, Leonie. "From the Campfire to the Computer: An Epistemology of Multiplicity and the Story Turn in Planning." *Multimedia Explorations in Urban Policy and Planning: Beyond the Flatlands*. Ed. Leonie Sandercock, Giovanni Attilli. Heidelberg: Springer, 2010. 17–37.

Rhythm & Repetition

1. Definition

Rhythm and repetition – established through sequences of words or recurring sound patterns – constitute the grid from which affective and imaginative world-building in language can emerge. Such sequences are the literary equivalents of the building blocks of an urban environment. They are the aesthetic material of prose and poetry, combing audio-visual form (more recognizable in sound than in sight) with fragments of meaning and purpose, as well as with symbolic function.

2. Example

In the urban built environment, the equivalent of these rhythmic patterns is to be found in sequences of material objects as well as series of standardized events that city dwellers will be able to perceive as both distinctive and coherent patterns (see fig. 14). Rhythm in urban planning is thus best described as the finding of a cadence, a contour, a figure of periodicity or pleasing combination of repetition and variation that establishes recognizability as well as harmony, while simultaneously promising to offer a solution to a recurring problem – to be applied in vastly distinctive urban scenarios around the globe. Building on the insights of Christopher Alexander's *Pattern Language*[74], the language of urban design has sought to use rhythm and repetition more systematically: Alexander's insight that some basic design ideas are virtually universal and can, with variation and adaptation to local context, be applied to solve recurring design challenges, is reminiscent of the idea of rhythm as repetition with variation as it exists in poetry.

Fig. 14: Sequence of arches in a tunnel. Lührmannstraße, Essen.

Photo by Phillip James Grider

3. Explanation

Rhythm arguably conjoins spatial, temporal and energetic forces. It emerges from the coincidence of repetition, interference and the cycle of "birth, growth, peak, then decline and end".[75] Here, it might help to think that rhythm and repetition also belong to the oldest and most important systematic devices of literary expression, which organize certain aspects of phonology for aesthetic purposes. Material ordered in this way has pervasive effects on all other levels of poetic language – morphology, syntax, discourse.

By way of explanation, one of the operations needed for the production of poetic rhythm – meter – selects one phonological feature of language and its intonational features (stress, pitch, length) and reduces the existing complexity of stress in ordinary speech (3 to 4 levels of stress; high, medium and low pitch, various durations) to simple binary oppositions – stress vs. unstress; level vs. inflected pitch; long vs. short – which may be generalized as marked vs. unmarked. Regular patterns of these contrastive features create units of structure (feet, measures, metra, cola) that will in turn comprise the line of verse. Metrical rules do not themselves derive from the language in which they are used. Rather, they derive from general laws of rhythmicity and from arbitrary poetic conventions, which have developed over time. Generally, rhythm is defined by the five elements of regularity, repetition, variation, hierarchy and grouping.[76]

In poetry, it is the recurrence of stresses and pauses that is the most obvious path toward rhythm. Meter provides structure – the ideal, regular pattern of stressed syllables and unstressed syllables, whereas rhythm fills the grid, providing movement and variation within that structure. Meter and rhythm appear to be comparable to a theory and its praxis, which stand in productive tension to one another. Because some lines require the promotion of usually unstressed syllables or the demotion of usually stressed syllables in order to fulfil metric requirements, whereas other lines are marked by incomplete feet, meters or lines, it seems most likely that the actual rhythms playfully work against a theoretical meter, which is recognizable to experienced readers as soon as little more than 25% of all lines in a given poem follow the ideal metrical pattern.[77]

Notions of space syntax usually claim that architecture, much like poetry, gives sensual access to human patterns and thus allows a critical reflection on the forms and buildings in which human beings make themselves at home.

4. Applications

When thinking about rhythm and repetition, it is helpful to think of words as building blocks of the imagination and of the world to be seen. Words are potentially not transparent but rather opaque, since they are given figured and textured shape. Humans are not only producing patterns, they are also projecting them as they go along. Paul Fussell speaks of a "contract between poet and reader" which rather narrowly prescribes the recognition of patterns of sound and language.[78] This idea of a contract between designer / planner and user indicates that the prerequisites of sustainable patterns of rhythm and repetition consist of extensive negotiations and mutual consent. Having always worked with the rules of rhythm in the material world – recurring building blocks, housing patterns, and vistas – planners, in thinking about rhythm and repetition, are encouraged to think beyond the material city. Equally important are the repetition and variation of immaterial and imaginary elements: the use of urban functions (including unintended functions), or of references to the city's palimpsestic history or to real and imaginary cities relevant for the planning area.

Related entries: Model, Path-dependency, Scripts, Symbol

Further Reading

Hillier, Bill. *Space is the Machine: A Configurational Theory of Architecture*. UCL: Space Syntax, 2004.

Levine, Caroline. *Forms: Whole, Rhythm, Hierarchy, Network*. Princeton: Princeton University Press, 2015.

Opondo, Sam Okoth. "Genre and the African City: The Politics and Poetics of Urban Rhythms." *Journal for Cultural Research* 12, no. 1 (2008): 59–79. DOI: 10.1080/14797580802090984.

Scenario

1. Definition

A scenario, especially in the field of future studies[79], is a description of a potential future development, usually presented in the form of alternative possible developments. A scenario can be merely sketched or fully developed.

2. Example

Research on the future of urban mobility frequently works with different scenarios. To take one example from the Ruhr region, these may include, for instance, alternative versions of the future in which **(1)** rapid technological innovation will have led to largely automated mobility systems ('smart mobility'), **(2)** a concern with human health and well-being will have led to an emphasis on walkability, bikeability and electrically-powered public transport with an inner-city ban on fossil-fuel vehicles ('healthy city'), **(3)**, inhospitable living conditions in cities will have led to deurbanization, or **(4)** the present-day situation continues as it is (commonly referred to as 'business as usual'). Frequently, there is also a scenario that combines elements of the other scenarios **(5)**. Each of these scenarios may be outlined in a short text accompanied by suggestive visualisations (see fig. 15).

Fig. 15: Scenarios for future urban mobility and settlement patterns originally developed for Germany's Ruhr region. A frequently formulated scenario not visualized here is one in which drastic environmental degradation will have led to the enforced imposition of radical measures ('eco-dictatorship').

Source: Institute of City Planning and Urban Design, University of Duisburg-Essen. Used by permission

Fully developed scenarios focus on turning points and on chains of causality that lead up to particular futures. They are often structured around powerful metaphors, which tend to be used in titles of particular scenarios ('smart city', 'healthy city') to describe but also to make a rhetorical argument for particular possible worlds, and for the decisions that will lead to a chosen future. The presentation of alternative futures side by side tends to be a potent way to engage readers, who are drawn into the imagined storyworld to consider the 'what if' of possible developments. It also suggests a degree of impartiality – after all, alternative scenarios suggest that readers are allowed to make up their own mind about the desirability or feasibility of particular futures. In most cases, the way the scenarios are presented guides the reader towards one or two of them. Thus, the 'business as usual' scenario in the example above is presented in a distinctively negative light.

3. Explanation

The development of scenario techniques can be traced to military strategies during the Cold War, with Herman Kahn of the RAND Corporation combining game theory and fictional stories to devise possible strategies in the face of nuclear threats. An awareness of possible future developments and their impacts on a given system (a city, a region, the nation state, the planet as a whole) is clearly crucial to any responsible and circumspect planning and strategy development. Two distinct methods used in scenarios are back-casting and forecasting. While forecasting starts out with the present and extrapolates developments towards the future, back-casting tends to start out from an imagined desirable future and then tracks the possible pathways capable of leading to that future from our present day – a method that is close to what happens when we read science fiction or near-future utopian literature (such as Edward Bellamy's 1888 utopian novel *Looking Backward*). The development of future scenarios and the testing of alternative parameter settings in terms of their impact on a given system are an important bridge between literature and planning. One of the functions of literature is that it serves as a form of symbolic action, as a social experiment free from the constraints of everyday life – literature as 'depragmatised behaviour in rehearsal', which makes it possible symbolically to try out in fiction different scenarios or potential solutions for key societal issues. A classic formulation is Dieter Wellershoff's, who spoke of literature as a "space of simulation for alternative behaviour in rehearsal at reduced risk".[80] However, literary texts frequently do not attempt to solve a problem by imposing an answer – and even if they do, they are often less interesting for the answer they propose than for having asked the question and providing some insights into what is at stake. In this, of course, literary texts differ greatly from planning documents.

4. Applications

The most important contribution of alternative scenarios might lie in their narrative characteristics: more elaborate scenarios can give insights into the complex storyworlds and values that underlie possible decisions. Moreover, future scenarios that draw on literary fiction could give some insights into what a particular possible future might actually feel like, for example by including narrative characters – a way to envision the future as already inhabited by people with real senses and affects, rather than envisioning the future as a blank slate waiting to be colonized.[81] One specific type of working with scenarios at the intersection between planning studies and literary/cultural studies is research on the potential role of science fiction for planning.[82]

In addition to allowing for more informed decision-making, scenarios also have a purpose in the context of planning with uncertainty. Climate research, for instance, has long realized the need to think in terms of scenarios rather than pretending that developments can be predicted with a high degree of certainty. Different scenarios – whether for demographic developments, climate change and environmental degradation or different technological developments – can also help urban planners to decide what would be meaningful choices ('What would we be doing anyway? What would be helpful under any circumstances?'). Thinking in terms of scenarios might help planners to become aware of path-dependencies and to remain aware that the potential closure provided by one plan may be the origin of a new planning problem. Scenario techniques can thus aid in developing potentially reversible planning solutions in and for conditions of uncertainty.

Related entries: Closure, Future Narratives, Path-dependency, Scripts

Further Reading

Ameel, Lieven. *The Narrative Turn in Urban Planning: Plotting the Helsinki Waterfront*. New York: Routledge, 2021.

Gurr, Jens Martin. *Charting Literary Urban Studies: Texts as Models of and for the City*. New York: Routledge, 2021. 125–140. [open access, https://doi.org/10.4324/9781003111009].

Sandercock, Leonie. "From the Campfire to the Computer: An Epistemology of Multiplicity and the Story Turn in Planning." *Multimedia Explorations in Urban Policy and Planning: Beyond the Flatlands*. Ed. Leonie Sandercock, Giovanni Attili. Heidelberg/London/New York: Springer, 2010. 17–37.

Scripts

1. Definition

In the conctext of planning, a script is a suggestive recipe for urban development that combines a self-description or self-positioning as well as a plausible path from the past through the present and into the future, all packaged into a compelling story. For their persuasiveness, scripts frequently rely on an oscillation between descriptive and prescriptive components. Many globally current recipes or blueprints for urban development – from the 'sustainable city' through the 'creative city' to the 'smart city' – can best be understood as 'scripts'.

2. Example

In 2017, the city of Essen was the European Green Capital. The first paragraph of the application for the title submitted to the European Commission in 2014 states:

> From green to grey to green: The successful 150-year transformation story, from a city of coal and steel to the greenest city in North Rhine-Westphalia, is a role model of structural change for many cities in Europe. [...] Green infrastructure is the motor for our sustainable urban development. [...] The people's 'ability to change' is the key to the success of this process of transformation.

This brief passage (1) provides a self-description of Essen as a city in structural transformation, which today has become remarkably 'green', (2) invokes the knowledge about the hardships and challenges of structural transformation and (3) tells a story which makes plausible a development from the past into the present and suggests a way into the future, all combined into the kernel narrative "from green to grey to green", encapsulating the 150-year transformation from pre-industrial "green" via industrial "grey" to the post-industrial "green" city. This combination of self-description, process knowledge and the suggestive invocation of a future-oriented development, rendered in a mini-narrative, is a prototypical example of a 'script'.

3. Explanation

The notion of scripts in urban development combines descriptive as well as prescriptive definitions of the term from a range of fields and disciplines (including literary studies, social psychology, law, biblical scholarship, and artificial intelligence research). Thus, the notion of a script as the "typescript of a cinema or television film; the text of a broadcast announcement, talk, play, or other material"[83] already contains the more descriptive sense of a transcript, but also the prescriptive sense of an instruction to be carried out, of a pre-defined sequence of actions and dialogues appropriate in a specific setting. In a related sense originating in artificial intelligence research, a "script" is defined as as "a standard event sequence"[84] and as a form of procedural knowledge. The classical example of the restaurant script states that going to a restaurant involves a fairly fixed sequence of actions: sitting down, choosing from the menu, ordering, eating, paying the bill, leaving. Based on this notion, "script" also came to be used to refer to cultural models as powerful unconscious or semi-conscious guides of individual and collective human behaviour.[85]

The sense in which the term script is defined in social psychology as referring to "generic schemata of social events"[86] and to "symbolic and nonverbal elements in an organized and time-bound sequence of conduct through which persons both envision future behaviour and check on the quality of ongoing conduct"[87] combines the descriptive sense of a script as procedural knowledge, as well as a more prescriptive sense of appropriateness and social control. In the related psychological field of transaction analysis, script is the term used for the study of unconscious life plans developed in response to education and early experiences, plans that can be made conscious and can to some extent be rescripted or at least modified.[88] Transferred to cities, this notion suggests that path dependencies do play a significant role but that there is nonetheless no complete determinism. Finally, the notion also resonates with the related term scripture in the sense of Holy Scripture and suggests a piece of writing with a claim to authority or one that is perceived as being sanctified or beyond critique.

A script can be understood, then, as a combination of procedural knowledge, self-description and blueprint for future development, based on an understanding of a city's past and its potentials (see fig. 16). Scripts thus oscillate between *descriptive* and *prescriptive* components. In keeping with the notion that scripts can be modified, planners and city officials have frequently sought to change the script behind their cities' development, for instance by describing a way forward for postindustrial cities in the U.S. rustbelt, the German Ruhr region or the English Midlands.

In the field of urban planning, Christopher Alexander's notion of "patterns" can be seen as a closely related concept: Here, a pattern is a modular solution, blueprint or recipe for a specific design challenge, a solution that can be replicated or adapted in comparable contexts to address comparable problems.[89] This notion of a hierarchically ordered system of patterns as a language – with a specific vocabulary, grammar and syntax and a formulaic way of outlining them, their contexts and applications – has been widely adopted as a travelling concept in other disciplines, most prominently in software engineering.[90]

Fig. 16: This 1920s advertising poster for Welwyn Garden City traces a path from "Yesterday: Living and Working in the Smoke" via "Today: Living in the Suburbs – Working in the Smoke" to "To-morrow: Living & Working in the Sun at Welwyn Garden City" and thus explicity frames a blueprint for urban development as a path from a dark past into a bright future.

Source: 1920s advertisement for Welwyn Garden City; Monclús and Díez Medina 19[91]

Scripts in the way we understand them are also inherently performative: If persuasive enough, they bring about what they often merely purport to describe. If a way to do things is described as being pervasive in a large number of cities, this may lead other cities to pursue similar policies. This is particularly evident in the case of the creative city script as outlined and promoted by Richard Florida: While in parts allegedly *describing* a pattern of urban development – the accumulation of the so-called creative class in particularly attractive locations offering the "three T's" of "Talent", "Technology" and "Tolerance"[92] – these standardized "creative fixes"[93] quickly became a blueprint and recipe for cities to follow, rolled out in numerous consulting projects by Florida himself and by global consulting firms in his wake. The characteristic oscillation between description and prescription inherent to scripts led to a self-reinforcing global hype of urban development strategies geared towards the attraction of the desirable creative class segment.

These multi-authored, multi-interest scripts operate along the literary lines of epic, tragic, and melodramatic patterns and conventions. If, for instance, urban development narratives are formulated in terms of growth, agency or attainment of potential, then these are the generic terms of the 19th-century *Bildungsroman* as the narrative of emergent self-confidence and agency.[94]

4. Applications

The frequently scripted nature of blueprints for urban development relies on narrative acts, generic formula, rhetorical strategies, personification, metaphors and visualizations and other profoundly literary devices. Several globally pertinent patterns of urban development can be understood as scripts: For instance, waterfront redevelopment, and the transformation of former port areas into upmarket residential or mixed-use districts – with iconic early examples in New York City's waterfronts or the London Docklands – has long been a globally circulating blueprint. Although this development can simply be seen a case of similar (obvious) solutions to the identical challenge of finding new uses for abandoned former port areas in potentially attractive locations on the water, such an understanding significantly underestimates the impact of powerful narrative and visual strategies, leading to remarkably similar iconographies of successful development, frequently with virtually interchangable architecture in very different locations. The concept of 'scripts' can thus also help to understand the global diffusion of recent and current models of urban development.

Related entries: Future Narratives, Genre, Narrative, Path-dependency, Scenario, Travelling Models

Further Reading

Buchenau, Barbara, Jens Martin Gurr. "'Scripts' in Urban Development: Procedural Knowledge, Self-Description and Persuasive Blueprint for the Future." Jens Martin Gurr. *Charting Literary Urban Studies: Texts as Models of and for the City*. New York: Routledge, 2021. 141–163 [open access: https://www.taylorfrancis.com/chapters/oa-edit/10.4324/9781003111009-8]

Herman, David. "Scripts, Sequences, and Stories: Elements of a Postclassical Narratology." *Literary Theory: An Anthology*. Ed. Julie Rivkin, Michael Ryan. Chichester: Wiley Blackwell, 2017. 230–247.

Katzenberg, Chris, Kornelia Freitag. "Scripting the Inclusive City, Narrating the Self: Contemporary Rust Belt Memoirs in Poetry and Prose." *City Scripts: Narratives of Postindustrial Urban Futures*. Ed. Barbara Buchenau, Jens Martin Gurr, Maria Sulimma. Columbus: Ohio State University Press, forthcoming.

Travelling Models

1. Definition

Travelling models are blueprints for urban development – such as 'waterfront revitalization', the 'eco-city', the 'creative city' or the 'smart city'– that come to be implemented globally or at least across different regions within a comparatively short period of time. Such blueprints are frequently, though not always, promoted by globally operating tech companies, consultancies or investors and are frequently publicized and diffused by means of suggestive narratives, attractive visualizations and promises of economic prosperity, sustainability and/or lifestyle benefits to consumers and residents.

2. Example

Richard Florida's account of the role of the so-called "creative class" in urban development – allegedly manifested in technological and social innovation, job creation and increased tax revenues – in his 2005 book *Cities and the Creative Class* within a few years led to a global flurry of cities developing strategies to attract such talents, frequently with the help of consulting projects rolled out by a handful of globally operating experts and consulting firms. In the wake of these projects, urban development in many cities openly promoted strategies designed to attract desirable segments of the population defined in terms of their potential role in the economic development of cities. Frequent side effects were an instrumentalization of art and artists as mere location factors in the generation of an attractively hip city image as well as gentrification-like processes in the wake of such urban development strategies.

3. Explanation

Recent decades have seen an unprecedented global diffusion of ideas, recipes and blueprints for urban development, many of which can be subsumed under a fairly limited number of labels such as smart, sustainable, creative, and socially inclusive urban development. Under the headings of policy mobility, policy diffusion or institutional transplant/transfer, this phenomenon has attracted an enormous amount of scholarly attention in various disciplines.[95] Despite different guiding questions and preoccupations, these various traditions share an interest in identifying factors that may enable or impede successful transfers. Research on contextual factors has long assumed that similar political or legal systems, common linguistic and cultural traditions and conventions, or other – broadly speaking – cultural similarities might make successful policy transfers more likely. However, there is strong empirical evidence against such assumptions.[96] Most policy mobility research has neglected the extent to which such blueprints for urban development frequently rely on storytelling, suggestive visualization, personification and other strategies of generating persuasiveness.[97]

We can further observe that many documents central to urban policy mobility, by being referred to as toolkits, manuals or blueprints in their titles, already announce their suitability for rollout and virtually global implementation. Such packages, however, are rarely 'plug and play', but frequently need to be customised and adapted in consulting projects, for which freely available brochures, rankings, survey papers, etc. merely function as appetisers. For instance, consultancy firm Copenhagenize Design Co. publishes a freely accessible index of bicycle-friendly cities and then sells manuals and consulting projects on how to 'copenhagenize' a city, i.e. how to become as bicycle-friendly as the long-term number one city in such rankings, Copenhagen.[98] The use of travelling models to copenhagenise contemporary cities has received a fair amount of criticism, most poignantly by Darran Anderson in *Imaginary Cities*:

> We can Copenhagenise our future cities, make them as green and smart as we can, but provided we are still embedded in systems that reward cronyism, exploitation and short-term profiteering, that require poverty and degradation, it will be mere camouflage. Dystopias will have cycle lanes and host World Cups. What may save us is, in Orwell's words, a dedication to 'common decency', and the perpetual knowledge that it need not be like this.[99]

4. Applications

Several globally prevalent patterns of urban development function as traveling models. One prominent example of a pervasive recent travelling model is that of the ubiqitous smart city (see fig. 17). Promoted largely by global tech companies such as IBM, Cisco, Google, Samsung or Siemens, such developments – whether in Korea, China, the U.S., Canada or different European countries – are frequently marketed with utopian promises of residential comfort, liveability, safety and sustainability, often intersecting with eco-city concepts.[100]

All in all, we can observe a fairly limited set of globally prevalent urban development models, the vast majority of which fall under the headings of the green or sustainable city, the smart city, the competitive/prosperous/growing city and, more recently, and with less corporate backing, the inclusive city. These few recipes frequently overlap or appear in combination. As merely one example, the Asian Development Bank in 2012 announced "Green Cities", "Inclusive Cities" and "Competitive Cities" as the "three major themes of [its work] in the urban sector over the coming years".[101] The combinations are frequently promoted with little reflection on their potentially conflicting nature. For instance, the greening of neighborhoods frequently comes at the expense of social inclusiveness, a phenomenon that has come to be known as environmental gentrification.

Fig. 17: The model of the smart city has become one of the most pervasive travelling concepts on contemporary urban development. Seen here is the 'Smart City Nansha' in Guangzhou, China.

Source : https ://commons.wikimedia.org/wiki/File :Smart_City_Nansha.jpg

Related entries: Model, Scripts

Further Reading

Bal, Mieke. *Travelling Concepts in the Humanities: A Rough Guide*. Toronto: University of Toronto Press, 2002.

Datta, Ayona, Nancy Odendaal. "Smart Cities and the Banality of Power." *Environment and Planning D* 37, no. 3 (2019): 387–392.

Gurr, Jens Martin. "From the 'Garden City' to the 'Smart City': Literary Urban Studies, Policy Mobility Research and Travelling Urban Models." Jens Martin Gurr. *Charting Literary Urban Studies: Texts as Models of and for the City*. New York: Routledge, 2021. 164–194.

Hatavara, Mari, Lars-Christer Hydén, Matti Hyvärinen, eds. *The Travelling Concepts of Narrative*. Amsterdam: John Benjamins, 2013.

Utopia

1. Definition

Utopia is the depiction of a non-existing, imagined state or place, in which one finds crystallized a vision of the 'good society'. This conceptualization of an ideal societal form can be expressed either in a literary narrative, or in the more rationalistic account of a philosophical treatise. A utopian state is typically located in a more or less inaccessible place, distanced from the reader in place and time. Utopian environments have been situated in outer space, or within a hollow earth, on allegedly remote islands or in a distant past or future. Within this variety of settings, the form of the city has had a continuous appeal as the preferred spatial form.[102]

2. Example

In a little-known utopian text, Edward E. Hale's *Sybaris and Other Homes* (1869), an American adventurer enters a Greek city that has been miraculously preserved in a secretive spot on the Italian coast. The strange city exemplifies a number of interesting urban planning solutions with reference also to lively debates on cities and urbanity in the US at the time. Sybaris is organized as a horizontal utopia; all buildings have only one storey, and "stair-builders … are forbidden to live in Sybaris by … fundamental law".[103] The result is a landscape in which the distinctions between suburb and the centre have been erased, in part made possible by a network of public transport by cable car. The visit to Sybaris is in effect an introduction to a suburban dream city, in which "a house without its own garden was an abomination, and easy communication with the suburbs was a necessity."[104] The meaning of this utopian text stems in large part from its comparison with the bleak working-class living conditions in contemporary Boston, which feature in a separate short story in the book.

3. Explanation

Ideas of the ideal society and the ideal city have always informed urban planning and policy, from Plato's *Republic* (4th century BC) to Thomas More's *Utopia* (1516) and Edward Bellamy's *Looking Backward* (1888). But utopian thinking has become increasingly suspect in the course of the twentieth century, in literature, planning and policy. *Looking Backward* has been read as "a sinister blueprint of tyranny"[105] and Plato's *Republic* as "the prototype of the fascist state".[106] The negative associations of utopia are primarily related to its characteristics of being fixed and essentially authoritarian. Utopia is the envisioning of an ideal state, and tends to project a fixed and final end-state of things, the very opposite of the real city which is never complete or finished.

Any planner working with utopia today runs the risk of being called naïve, or may be suspected of hiding dark aims when proposing a form of utopia as solution to urban challenges. And yet projects such as the King Abdullah Economic City (KAEC) in Jeddah, Saudi Arabia (evoked in Dave Eggers' *A Hologram for a King*, 2012); *Torontopia*, a distinctively utopian vision of future Toronto, or the island Utopia in Dutch city Almere – an artificial island in an artificial lake on an artificial island in an artificial lake, and one of the sites to host the 2022 Floriade World Exhibition – shows that utopian naming and utopian visionary practices have not run out of steam regardless of claims that we are living in post-utopian times.

Fig. 18: Frederick Law Olmsted's curvilinear vision (1869) for Riverside, Illinois, visible here on a 1950 census map. U.S. National Archives and Records Administration.

https://commons.wikimedia.org/wiki/File:1950_Census_Enumeration_District_Maps_-_Illinois_(IL)_-_Cook_County_-_Riverside_-_ED_16-380_to_391_-_NARA_-_12013499.jpg

In the case of Hale's account of Sybaris, this was a text that provided an indirect influence for Frederick Law Olmsted's plans for Riverside, Illinois, planned in the late 1860s and one of the early examples of American suburban city planning. Riverside was the "best-known curvilinear suburb of the nineteenth century", and its plan contains an abundance of pastorally curving streets.[107] Olmsted and Hale corresponded with each other after Olmsted had read *Sybaris and Other Homes*, and when Hale visited Riverside, he "there found his Sybaris fully realised".[108] Riverside was not an unequivocal success: inhabitants found it extremely difficult to orient themselves in the curving, disorienting streets (see fig. 18). In more general terms, the drive for suburbanization led to the new urban problems of sprawl, inner city decay, car-dependency and unsustainable practices.

4. Applications

What utopia can still bring to planning is not authoritarian illusions of the good city in its definitive form. But utopia can bring a sense of "necessary dreaming" to planning.[109] Important for thinking about the value of utopia in twenty-first century planning is the realization that literary utopia is never only about an idealized future, but always entails a critical view of the present. Utopia invites its audience to look with regret or at least a distinct lack of satisfaction to present flaws in urban design. Its focus is not necessarily on a perfect end-state, but on the imperfection of the present city, and the imperative to try to do better, whether it is in tackling questions of equity, just housing, sustainability, inclusion, or access to public space.

For a planner aiming to work with utopia, starting out from some of the key features of literary utopia may be one way to proceed: to think of a plan's accompanying text, or a future scenario, in terms of a narrative that features a main character who is introduced into a strange environment by a knowledgeable local guide. As the guide explains to the newcomer the secrets of this idealized city and society, the newcomer looks with new eyes to their home society, and the reader with them. The form of didactic dialogue typical of utopian narratives may in fact be particularly well suited to planning texts.

A focus on fixed and immovable end-states (characteristic of utopias) may lead to future visions of the city as being read as dystopias: as imagined perversions of an ideal state, against which the main character (or the reader) is set to rebel or from which they want to escape. One way to address this possible outcome is to think of a plan and accompanying texts not as imagined end-points but as the stepping stones for future rounds of planning and deliberation. One of the challenges of planning is to balance the tendency of planning towards idealized, closed views of the future city, and the need to allow for open-endedness, uncertainty, and flexibility.

Related entries: Ambiguity, Genre, Scenario

Further Reading

Ameel, Lieven. "Cities Utopian, Dystopian and Apocalyptic." *Palgrave Handbook of Literature and the City*. Ed. Jeremy Tambling. London: Palgrave, 2016. 785–800.

Kumar, Krishan. "The Ends of Utopia." *New Literary History* 41, no. 3 (2010): 549–569.

Pinder, David. *Visions of the City: Utopianism, Power and Politics in Twentieth-Century Urbanism*. New York: Routledge, 2002.

Wilson, Elizabeth. *The Sphinx in the City: Urban Life, the Control of Disorder, and Women*. London: Virago, 1991.

Works Cited

Abbott, H. Porter. "Closure." *Routledge Encyclopedia of Narrative Theory*. Ed. David Herman, Manfred Jahn, Marie-Laure Ryan. London: Routledge, 2010. 65–66.

Adhikari, Binay, Jianling Li. "Modelling Ambiguity in Urban Planning." *Annals of GIS* 19, no. 3 (2013): 143–152.

Alexander, Christopher, Sara Ishikawa, Murray Silverstein. *A Pattern Language: Towns, Buildings, Construction*. Oxford: Oxford University Press, 1977.

Ameel, Lieven. "Redemptive Scripts in the City Novel." *City Scripts: Narratives of Postindustrial Urban Futures*. Ed. Barbara Buchenau, Jens Martin Gurr, Maria Sulimma. Columbus: Ohio State University Press, forthcoming.

Ameel, Lieven. "'A Stream of Words' – The Antwerp Quay Poem as Interrogation of Urban Open Form, Polyphony, and Radical Dialogue." *Textual Practice* 36, no. 7 (2021): 1175–1194.

Ameel, Lieven. "Fraught Fictionality in Narratives of Future Catastrophe." *Narrative* 29, no. 3 (2021): 355–73.

Ameel, Lieven. *The Narrative Turn in Urban Planning: Plotting the Helsinki Waterfront*. New York: Routledge, 2021.

Ameel, Lieven. "Governing the Future: Perspectives from Literary Studies – Commentary to Jones." *Fennia* 197, no. 1 (2019): 145–148.

Ameel, Lieven. "A *Bildungsroman* for a Waterfront Development: Literary Genre and the Planning Narratives of Jätkäsaari, Helsinki." *Journal of Urban Cultural Studies* 3, no. 2 (2016): 167–187.

Ameel, Lieven. "Cities Utopian, Dystopian and Apocalyptic." *Palgrave Handbook of Literature and the City*. Ed. Jeremy Tambling. London: Palgrave, 2016. 785–800.

Ameel, Lieven. "Emplotting Urban Regeneration: Narrative Strategies in the Case of Kalasatama, Helsinki." *Re-City. Future City – Combining Disciplines*. Ed. Juho Rajaniemi. *DATUTOP* 34 (2016): 223–241.

Ameel, Lieven. "Narrative Mapping and Polyphony in Urban Planning." *Yhdyskuntasuunnittelu / Finnish Journal for Urban Studies* 2 (2016): 20–40.

Ameel, Lieven. "Towards a Narrative Typology of Urban Planning Narratives for, in, and of Planning in Jätkäsaari, Helsinki." *Urban Design International* 22, no. 4 (2016): 318–330.

Anderson, Darran. *Imaginary Cities*. London: Influx Press, 2015.

Antwerp. *Tussen stad en stroom. Het Masterplan Scheldekaaien Antwerpen*. Antwerp: GSA, 2011.

Aristotle, Longinus, Demetrius. *Aristotle: Poetics. Longinus: On the Sublime. Demetrius: On Style*. Translated by Stephen Halliwell, W. Hamilton Fyfe, Doreen C. Innes, W. Rhys Roberts. Revised by Donald A. Russell. Loeb Classical Library 199. Cambridge, MA: Harvard University Press, 1995.

Arnstein, Sherry J. "A Ladder of Citizen Participation." *Journal of the American Planning Association* 35, no. 4 (1969): 216–224.

Asian Development Bank. *Green Cities*. Ed. Michael Lindfield, Florian Steinberg. Urban Development Series. Mandaluyong City, Philippines: Asian Development Bank 2012.

Attridge. Derek. "Rhythm." *The Princeton Encyclopedia of Poetry and Poetics*. Ed. Roland Greene et al. Princeton: Princeton University Press, 2012. 1195–1198.

Augé, Marc. *Non-Places: Introduction to an Anthropology of Supermodernity*. Transl. by John Howe. London: Verso, 1995 (Original: 1992).

Bakhtin, Mikhail. *Problems of Dostoevsky's Poetics*. Minneapolis: University of Minnesota Press, 1984.

Bal, Mieke. *Travelling Concepts in the Humanities: A Rough Guide*. Toronto: University of Toronto Press, 2002.

Batty, Michael. "Can it Happen Again? Planning Support, Lee's Requiem and the Rise of the Smart Cities Movement." *Environment and Planning B: Planning and Design* 41 (2014): 388–391.

Batty, Michael. *The New Science of Cities*. Boston: MIT Press, 2013.

BBSR – Bundesinstitut für Bau-, Stadt- und Raumforschung. *Von Science-Fiction-Städten lernen: Szenarien für die Stadtplanung*. Bonn: BBSR, 2015 [https://www.bbsr.bund.de/BBSR/DE/veroeffentlichungen/sonderveroeffentlichungen/2015/science-fiction-staedte.html].

Bell, Wendell. *Foundations of Futures Studies: History, Purposes, and Knowledge*. London: Routledge, 1997/2003.

Benjamin, Walter. *The Arcades Project*. Trans. Howard Eiland, Kevin McLaughlin. Cambridge, MA: The Belknap Press of Harvard University Press, 1999.

Berne, Eric. *Transactional Analysis in Psychotherapy: A Systematic Individual and Social Psychiatry*. New York: Grove Press, 1961.

Berne, Eric. "Transactional Analysis: A New and Effective Method of Group Therapy." *American Journal of Psychotherapy* 12 (1958): 735–743.

Bibri, Simon Elias. *Advances in the Leading Paradigms of Urbanism and their Amalgamation: Compact Cities, Eco-Cities, and Data-Driven Smart Cities*. Cham: Springer, 2020.

Bird, Susan, Malin Fransberg, Vesa Peipinen. "Hot in Helsinki: Exploring Legal Geographies in a DIY Sauna." *Flinders Law Journal* 18 (2016): 377–397.

Bode, Christoph, Rainer Dietrich. *Future Narratives: Theory, Poetics, and Media-Historical Moment*. Berlin/Boston: de Gruyter, 2013.

Borosch, Juliane. "Changing the Metonymy: Michigan Central Station and the Face of Detroit." *U.S. American Culture as Popular Culture*. Ed. Astrid Böger, Florian Sedlmeier. American Studies Monograph Series 318. Universitätsverlag Winter, 2022. 403–423.

Borosch, Juliane, Barbara Buchenau. "Walking Down Woodward – (Re-)Telling a City's Stories through Urban Figures." *City Scripts: Narratives of Postindustrial Urban Futures*. Ed. Barbara Buchenau, Jens Martin Gurr, Maria Sulimma. Columbus: Ohio State University Press, forthcoming.

te Brömmelstroet, Marco, Peter Pelzer, Stan Geertman. "Forty Years after Lee's Requiem: Are We Beyond the Seven Sins?" *Environment and Planning B: Planning & Design* 41, no. 3 (2014): 381–387.

Buchenau, Barbara, Jens Martin Gurr. "'Scripts' in Urban Development: Procedural Knowledge, Self-Description and Persuasive

Blueprint for the Future." Jens Martin Gurr. *Charting Literary Urban Studies: Texts as Models of and for the City*. New York: Routledge, 2021. 141–163.

Buchenau, Barbara, Jens Martin Gurr. "On the Textuality of American Cities and their Others: A Disputation." *Projecting American Studies: Essays on Theory, Method, and Practice*. Ed. Frank Kelleter, Alexander Starre. Heidelberg: Winter, 2018. 135–152.

Buchenau, Barbara, Jens Martin Gurr. "Urban American Studies and the Conjunction of Textual Strategies and Spatial Processes." *Spaces—Communities—Representations: Urban Transformations in the USA*. Ed. Julia Sattler. Bielefeld: transcript, 2016. 395–420.

Buchenau, Barbara, Jens Martin Gurr, Maria Sulimma, eds. *City Scripts: Narratives of Postindustrial Urban Futures*. Columbus: Ohio State University Press, forthcoming.

Busse, Beatrix, Jennifer Smith, Ingo H. Warnke. "Declaring Places, Placing Declaratives – An Introduction." *Place-Making in the Declarative City*. Ed. Beatrix Busse, Ingo H. Warnke, Jennifer Smith. Berlin/Boston: de Gruyter, 2020. 1–14. https://doi.org/10.1515/9783110634754-001.

Butler, Martin, Jens Martin Gurr. "Urbane Populärkultur als Bewertungspraxis und -ressource: Zum normativen Potential populärkultureller Inszenierung und diskursiver Aneignung urbaner Räume." *Place-Making in urbanen Diskursen*. Ed. Ingo H. Warnke, Beatrix Busse. Berlin/München/Boston: de Gruyter, 2014. 369–384.

Carney, George O. "Music and Place." *The Sounds of People and Places. A Geography of American Music from Country to Classical and Blues to Bop*. Ed. George O. Carney. Lanham: Rowman & Littlefield, ^{4}2003. 203–216.

Condello, Annette. *The Architecture of Luxury*. Farnham: Ashgate, 2014.

Copenhagenize Design Co. "The 20 Most Bike-Friendly Cities on the Planet, Ranked." 2019. https://copenhagenizeindex.eu.

Courage, Cara, Tom Borrup, Maria Rosario Jackson, Kylie Legge, Anita McKeown, Louise Platt, Jason Schupbach, eds. *The Routledge Handbook of Placemaking*. London/New York: Routledge, 2021.

Cresswell, Tim. "Weeds, Plagues, and Bodily Secretions: A Geographical Interpretation of Metaphors of Displacement." *Annals of the Association of American Geographers* 87, no. 2 (1997): 330–345.

Cugurullo, Federico. "The Origin of the Smart City Imaginary: From the Dawn of Modernity to the Eclipse of Reason." *The Routledge Companion to Urban Imaginaries*. Ed. Christoph Lindner, Miriam Meissner. New York: Routledge, 2019. n.p. https://www.taylorfrancis.com/books/e/9781315163956.

Datta, Ayona, Nancy Odendaal. "Smart Cities and the Banality of Power." *Environment and Planning D* 37, no. 3 (2019): 387–392.

de Jouvenel, Bertrand. *The Art of Conjecture*. Transl. Nikita Lary. New York: Basic Books, 1967.

Dillon, Sarah. *The Palimpsest: Literature, Criticism, Theory*. New York: Continuum, 2007.

Donoghue, Denis. *Metaphor*. Cambridge, MA: Harvard University Press, 2014.

Finnegan, Ruth. *Tales of the City: A Study of Narrative and Urban Life*. Cambridge: Cambridge University Press, 1998.

Fischer, Frank, John Forester, eds. *The Argumentative Turn in Policy Analysis and Planning*. London: Duke University Press, 1993.

Florida, Richard. *Cities and the Creative Class*. New York: Routledge, 2005.

Florida, Richard. *The Rise of the Creative Class: And How It's Transforming Work, Leisure and Everyday Life*. New York: Basic Books, 2002.

Ford Motor Company. *Michigan Central*. 2022. https://michigancentral.com, last accessed Nov. 12, 2022.

Forester, John. *Critical Theory, Public Policy, and Planning Practice: Towards a Critical Pragmatism*. Albany: State University of New York Press, 1993.

Fowler, Alastair. *Kinds of Literature: An Introduction to the Theory of Genres and Modes*. Oxford: Oxford University Press, 1982.

Frye, Northrop. "Varieties of Literary Utopias." *Daedalus* 94, no. 2 (1965): 323–347.

Fussell, Paul. *Poetic Meter & Poetic Form*. London: McGraw, 1979.

Gabriel, Richard P. *Patterns of Software: Tales from the Software Community*. Oxford: Oxford University Press, 1996.

Gagnon, John H. "Scripts and the Coordination of Sexual Behaviour" [1974]. *The Interpretation of Desire: Essays in the Study of Sexuality*. Ed. Gagnon. Chicago: Chicago University Press, 2004. 59–87.

Gould, Peter. "On Mental Maps." Discussion Paper No. 9. Michigan Interuniversity Community of Mathematical Geographers. Ann Arbor: University of Michigan, 1966.

Griem, Julika, Jo Reichertz, eds. *Mehr als Storytelling. Erzählen in den Geistes- und Sozialwissenschaften*. Bielefeld: transcript, 2022.

Gurr, Jens Martin. "Palimpsest." *The Routledge Companion to Literary Urban Studies*. Ed. Lieven Ameel. New York/London: Routledge, 2023. 72–86.

Gurr, Jens Martin. *Charting Literary Urban Studies: Texts as Models of and for the City*. New York: Routledge, 2021. 125–140 [open access, https://doi.org/10.4324/9781003111009].

Gurr, Jens Martin. "Reversing Perspectives: Urban Memory in Built and Literary Post-Industrial Cities." Gurr. *Charting Literary Urban Studies: Texts as Models of and for the City*. New York: Routledge, 2021. 84–109 [open access, https://doi.org/10.4324/9781003111009].

Gurr, Jens Martin. "Narrative Path Dependencies: From Scenario Building in Literary Texts to the Narratology and Rhetoric of Pragmatic Texts." Gurr. *Charting Literary Urban Studies: Texts as Models of and for the City*. New York: Routledge, 2021. 125–140 [open access, https://doi.org/10.4324/9781003111009].

Hale, Edward E. *Sybaris and Other Homes*. Boston: Fields, Osgood & Co, 1869.

Hansen, Hans. *Narrative Change: How Changing the Story Can Transform Society, Business, and Ourselves*. New York: Columbia University Press, 2020.

Harvey, David. "Contested Cities: Social Process and Spatial Form." *The City Reader*. Ed. Richard T. LeGates, Frederic Stout. London/New York: Routledge, [4]2000. 225–232.

Hassenpflug, Dieter. "Once Again: Can Urban Space be Read?" *Reading the City: Developing Urban Hermeneutics/Stadt lesen: Beiträge zu einer urbane Hermeneutik*. Ed. Dieter Hassenpflug, Nico Giersig, Bernhard Stratmann. Weimar: Verlag der Bauhaus-Universität, 2011. 49–58.

Hatavara, Mari, Lars-Christer Hydén, Matti Hyvärinen, eds. *The Travelling Concepts of Narrative*. Amsterdam: John Benjamins, 2013.

Healey, Patsy. "Planning in Relational Space and Time: Responding to New Urban Realities." *A Companion to the City*. Ed. Gary Bridge, Sophie Watson. Oxford: Blackwell, 2000. 517–530.

Hein, Carola, Dirk Schubert. "Resilience and Path Dependence: A Comparative Study of the Port Cities of London, Hamburg, and Philadelphia." *Journal of Urban History* 47, no. 2 (2021): 389–419.

Helsinki City. *Meri-Helsinki Yleiskaavassa*. Helsinki: City Planning Department, 2013.

Helsinki City. *Jätkäsaari osayleiskaava. Selostus*. Helsinki: City Planning Department, 2008.

Herman, David. "Scripts, Sequences, and Stories: Elements of a Postclassical Narratology." *Literary Theory: An Anthology*. Ed. Julie Rivkin, Michael Ryan. Chichester: Wiley Blackwell, 2017. 230–247.

Herman, David. *Basic Elements of Narrative*. Oxford: Wiley-Blackwell, 2009.

Hillier, Bill. *Space is the Machine: A Configurational Theory of Architecture*. UCL: Space Syntax, 2004.

Hillier, Jean. "Deconstructing the Discourse of Planning." *Explorations in Planning Theory*. Ed. Seymour J. Mandelbaum, Luigi Mazza, Robert W. Burchell. New Brunswick: Transaction Publishers, 1996. 289–298.

Holloway, Julian, James Kneale. "Mikhail Bakhtin: Dialogics of Space." *Thinking Space*. Ed. Mike Crang, Nigel Thrift. London: Routledge, 2000. 71–88.

Howard, Ebenezer. *Garden Cities of To-Morrow*. London: Swan Sonnenschein, 1902 [rev. 2nd ed. of Howard. *To-Morrow: A Peaceful Path to Real Reform*. London: Sonnenschein, 1898.

Iser, Wolfgang. *The Fictive and the Imaginary: Charting Literary Anthropology*. Baltimore: Johns Hopkins University Press, 1993.

Jacobs, Jane. *The Death and Life of Great American Cities*. New York: Random House, 1961.

Jain, Arun. "Urban Design Frameworks as a Basis for Development Strategies: A Portland Case Study." (2012). [open access, http://

mud-sala.sites.olt.ubc.ca/files/2015/08/Arun-Jain-UDFramewo rks-as-Basis-for-Development-Strategies.pdf].

Joss, Simon, Frans Sengers, Daan Schraven, Federico Caprotti, Youri Dayot. "The Smart City as Global Discourse: Storylines and Critical Junctures across 27 Cities." *Journal of Urban Technology* 26, no. 1 (2019): 3–34.

Jouvenel, Bertrand de. *The Art of Conjecture*. Transl. Nikita Lary. New York: Basic Books, 1967.

Katzenberg, Chris, Kornelia Freitag. "Scripting the Inclusive City, Narrating the Self: Contemporary Rust Belt Memoirs in Poetry and Prose." *City Scripts: Narratives of Postindustrial Urban Futures*. Ed. Barbara Buchenau, Jens Martin Gurr, Maria Sulimma. Columbus: Ohio State University Press, forthcoming.

Kermode, Frank. *The Sense of an Ending: Studies in the Theory of Fiction*. London: Oxford University Press, 1967.

Keunen, Bart. "Learning from Stories: Narrative Imagination in Urbanism." *Writingplace: Investigations in Architecture and Literature*. Ed. Klaske Havik, Jorge Mejía Hernández, Mike Schäfer, Mark Proosten, Susana Oliveira. Rotterdam: naio10 Publishers, 2016. 18–33.

Klein, Norman M. *The History of Forgetting: Los Angeles and the Erasure of Memory*. London: Verso, 1997/2008.

Koschorke, Albrecht. *Fact and Fiction: Elements of a General Theory of Narrative*. Transl. Joel Golb. Berlin/Boston: de Gruyter, 2018 [2012].

Kramsch, Olivier. "Tropics of Planning Discourse: Stalking the 'Constructive Imaginary' of Selected Urban Planning Histories." *Making the Invisible Visible: A Multicultural Planning History*. Ed. Leonie Sandercock. Berkeley: University of California Press, 1998. 163–183.

Kumar, Krishan. "The Ends of Utopia." *New Literary History* 41, no. 3 (2010): 549–569.

Labov, William, Joshua Waletzky. "Narrative Analysis: Oral Versions of Personal Experience." *Journal of Narrative and Life History* 7, no. 4 (1997) [^{1}1966]: 3–38.

Lakoff, George, Mark Johnson. *Metaphors We Live By*. Chicago: Chicago University Press, 2003 [1982].

Lalenis, Konstantinos, Martin de Jong, Virginie Mamadouh. "Families of Nations and Institutional Transplantation." *The Theory and Practice of Institutional Transplantation: Experiences with the Transfer of Policy Institutions*. Ed. de Jong, Mamadouh, Lalenis. Dordrecht: Kluwer Academic Publishers, 2002. 33–52.

Langdon, Philip. *A Better Place to Live: Reshaping the American Suburb*. Amherst: University of Massachusetts Press, 1994.

Lee, Douglass B. "Requiem for Large-Scale Models." *Journal of the American Institute of Planners* 39, no. 3 (1973): 163–178.

Lefebvre, Henri. *Éléments de rythmanalyse*. Paris: Éditions Syllepse, 1992. Translation: *Rhythmanalysis: Space, Time and Everyday Life*. London: Continuum, 2004.

LeSeur, Geta J. *Ten is the Age of Darkness: The Black Bildungsroman*. Columbia: University of Missouri Press, 1995.

Levine, Caroline. *Forms: Whole, Rhythm, Hierarchy, Network*. Princeton: Princeton University Press, 2015.

Löw, Martina. "The Intrinsic Logic of Cities: Towards a New Theory on Urbanism." *Urban Research & Practice* 5, no. 3 (2012): 303–315. DOI: 10.1080/17535069.2012.727545.

Loh, Carolyn G. et al. "Placemaking in Practice: Municipal Arts and Cultural Plans' Approaches to Placemaking and Creative Placemaking." *Journal of Planning Education and Research* (2022): n. pag. https://doi.org/10.1177/0739456X221100503.

Mäntysalo, Raina, Jonna K. Kangasoja, Vesa Kanninen. "The Paradox of Strategic Spatial Planning: A Theoretical Outline with a View on Finland." *Planning Theory & Practice* 16, no. 2 (2015): 169–183.

Mahr, Bernd. "Modelle und ihre Befragbarkeit: Grundlagen einer allgemeinen Modelltheorie." *Erwägen – Wissen – Ethik / Deliberation – Knowledge – Ethics: Forum für Erwägungskultur / Forum for Deliberative Culture* 26, no. 3 (2015): 329–342.

Massey, Doreen. "On Space and the City." *City Worlds*. Ed. John Allen, Doreen Massey, Steve Pile. London: Routledge, 1999. 151–174.

Mattila, Jorma J. "Kaikkien aikojen rakennusaalto käynnistyi Helsingissä." *Iltalehti*, September 12, 2008.

Meifert-Menhard, Felicitas. *Playing the Text, Performing the Future. Future Narratives in Print and Digiture*. Berlin/Boston: de Gruyter, 2013.

Monclús, Javier, Carmen Díez Medina. "Garden Cities and Garden Suburbs (1898–1930)." *Urban Visions: From Planning Culture to Landscape Urbanism*. Ed. Díez Medina, Monclús. Cham: Springer, 2018. 13–22.

Moretti, Franco. *The Way of the World: The Bildungsroman in European Culture*. London: Verso, 1987.

Mumford, Lewis. "Utopia, the City and the Machine." *Utopias and Utopian Thought*. Ed. Frank E. Manuel. Boston: Beacon Press, 1975 [^{1}1965]. 3–24.

Olesen, Kristian. "Talk to the Hand: Strategic Spatial Planning as Persuasive Storytelling of the Loop City." *European Planning Studies* 25, no. 6 (2017): 978–993.

Opondo, Sam Okoth. "Genre and the African City: The Politics and Poetics of Urban Rhythms." *Journal for Cultural Research* 12, no. 1 (2008): 59–79. DOI: 10.1080/14797580802090984.

Ossa-Richardson, Anthony. *A History of Ambiguity*. Princeton: Princeton University Press, 2019.

Pakarinen, Terttu. *Metaphors in Urban Planning: From Garden City to Zwischenstadt and Netzstadt*. Tampere: Tampere University of Technology, 2010.

Peck, Jamie. "Struggling with the Creative Class." *International Journal of Urban and Regional Research* 29, no. 4 (2005): 740–770.

Peck, Jamie, Nik Theodore. *Fast Policy: Experimental Statecraft at the Thresholds of Neoliberalism*. Minneapolis: University of Minnesota Press, 2015.

Phelan, James A. *Experiencing Fiction. Judgements, Progressions, and the Rhetorical Theory of Narrative*. Colombus: Ohio State University Press, 2007.

Pierson, Paul. "Increasing Returns, Path Dependence, and the Study of Politics." *The American Political Science Review* 94, no. 2 (2000): 251–267.

Pinder, David. "Necessary Dreaming: Uses of Utopia in Urban Planning." *The Ashgate Research Companion to Planning Theory*. Ed. Jean Hillier, Patsy Healey. Abingdon: Routledge, 2010. 343–364.

Pinder, David. *Visions of the City: Utopianism, Power and Politics in Twentieth-Century Urbanism*. New York: Routledge, 2002.

Quinn, Naomi, Dorothy Holland. "Culture and Cognition." *Cultural Models in Language and Thought*. Ed. Holland, Quinn. Cambridge: Cambridge University Press, 1987. 3–40.

Rabreau, Daniel. "City Planning." *Encyclopedia of the Enlightenment*. Ed. Michel Delon. Abingdon: Routledge, 2013. 256–262.

Ricœur, Paul. *Time and Narrative*. Chicago, IL: University of Chicago Press, [1984] 1990.

Rittel, Horst W. J., Melvin M. Webber. "Dilemmas in a General Theory of Planning." *Policy Sciences* 4, no. 2 (1973): 155–169.

Ryan, Marie-Laure. *A New Anatomy of Storyworlds. What Is, What If, As If*. Columbus: Ohio State University Press, 2022.

Ryan, Marie-Laure. "Narrative." *Routledge Encyclopedia of Narrative Theory*. Ed. David Herman, Manfred Jahn, Marie-Laure Ryan. London/New York: Routledge, 2005. 344–348.

Ryan, Marie-Laure. "Narrative in Real Time: Chronicle, Mimesis and Plot in the Baseball Broadcast." *Narrative* 1, no. 2 (1993): 138–155.

Ryan, Marie-Laure. "The Modes of Narrativity and their Visual Metaphors." *Style* 26, no. 3 (1992): 368–387.

Ryan, Marie-Laure, Kenneth Foote, Maoz Azaryahu. *Narrating Space, Spatializing Narrative: Where Narrative Theory and Geography Meet*. Columbus: Ohio University Press, 2016.

Sandercock, Leonie. "From the Campfire to the Computer: An Epistemology of Multiplicity and the Story Turn in Planning." *Multimedia Explorations in Urban Policy and Planning: Beyond the Flatlands*. Ed. Leonie Sandercock, Giovanni Attili. Heidelberg, London/New York: Springer, 2010. 17–37.

Schank, Roger C., Robert P. Abelson. *Scripts, Plans, Goals and Understanding: An Inquiry into Human Knowledge Structures*. Hillsdale: Lawrence Erlbaum, 1977.

Seitel, Peter. "Theorizing Genres – Interpreting Works." *New Literary History* 34, no. 2 (2003): 277–279.

Sennett, Richard. *The Conscience of the Eye: The Design and Social Life of Cities*. New York: W.W. Norton, 1992 [1990].

Sharp, Darren, Rob Raven. "Urban Planning by Experiment at Precinct Scale: Embracing Complexity, Ambiguity, and Multiplicity." *Urban Planning* 6, no. 1 (2021). DOI: https://doi.org/10.17645/up.v6i1.3525.

Shiller, Robert J. *Narrative Economics: How Stories Go Viral and Drive Major Economic Events*. Princeton: Princeton University Press, 2019.

Sidorkin, Alexander. "Carnival and Dialogue: Opening New Conversations." *Dialogue as a Means of Collective Communication*. Ed. Bela H. Banathy, Patrick M. Jenlink. New York: Springer, 2005. 277–288.

Söderström, Ola, Till Paasche, Francisco Klauser. "Smart Cities as Corporate Storytelling." *City* 18, no. 3 (2014): 307–320.

Stachowiak, Herbert. *Allgemeine Modelltheorie*. Wien/New York: Springer, 1973.

Star, Susan Leigh, James Griesemer. "Ecology, 'Translations' and Boundary Objects: Amateurs and Professionals in Berkeley's Museum of Vertebrate Zoology, 1907–39." *Social Studies of Science* 19, no. 3 (1989): 387–420.

Stigler, James W., James Hiebert. *The Learning Gap: Best Ideas from the World's Teachers for Improving Education in the Classroom*. New York: Free Press, 1999.

Suttles, Gerald D. "The Cumulative Texture of Local Urban Culture." *American Journal of Sociology* 90, no. 2 (1984): 283–304.

The City of New York (Bill de Blasio, Dominic Williams, Daniel A. Zarrilli). *OneNYC 2050. Building a Strong and Fair City*. Vol. 1. New York: NYC.GOV, 2019.

The City of New York (Michael R. Bloomberg, Amanda M. Burden). *Vision 2020. New York City Comprehensive Waterfront Plan*. New York: NYCPlanning, 2011.

Throgmorton, James A. "Storytelling and City Crafting in a Contested Age: One Mayor's Practice Story." *Planners in Politics: Do They Make a Difference?* Ed. Louis Albrechts. Cheltenham, UK: Edward Elgar Publications, 2020. 174–197.

Throgmorton, James A. "Planning as Persuasive Storytelling in a Global-Scale Web of Relationships." *Planning Theory* 2, no. 2 (2003): 125–35.

Throgmorton, James A. *Planning as Persuasive Storytelling: The Rhetorical Construction of Chicago's Electric Future*. Chicago: University of Chicago Press, 1996.

van Hulst, Merlijn. "Storytelling, a Model of and a Model for Planning." *Planning Theory* 11, no. 3 (2012): 299–318.

van Hulst, Merlijn, Haridimos Tsoukas. "Understanding Extended Narrative Sensemaking: How Police Officers Accomplish Story Work." *Organization* (July 3, 2021). Online first. https://doi.org/1 0.1177/13505084211026878.

Walter, Mareile. *Making Plans – Telling Stories: Planning in Karlskrona/ Sweden 1980–2010*. PhD; thesis, Blekinge Institute of Technology, 2013.

Wellershoff, Dieter. *Literatur und Lustprinzip*. Cologne: Kiepenheuer & Witsch, 1973.

White, Hayden. "The Value of Narrativity in the Representation of Reality." *On Narrative*. Ed. W.J.T. Mitchell. Chicago: University of Chicago Press, 1981. 1–24.

White, Hayden. "Introduction". *Metahistory: The Historical Imagination in 19th-Century Europe*. Baltimore: Johns Hopkins University Press, 1973. 1–42.

Whitney, Paul. "Schemas, Frames, and Scripts in Cognitive Psychology." *International Encyclopedia of the Social & Behavioral Sciences*. Ed. Neil J. Smelser, Paul Baltes. Oxford: Elsevier, 2001. 13522–13526.

Wiig, Alan. "IBM's Smart City as a Techno-utopian Policy Mobility." *City* 19, no. 2–3 (2015): 258–273.

Wilson, Elizabeth. *The Sphinx in the City: Urban Life, the Control of Disorder, and Women*. London: Virago, 1991.

Winslow, Rosemary Gates. "Meter." *The Princeton Encyclopedia of Poetry and Poetics*. Ed. Roland Greene et al. Princeton: Princeton University Press, ^{4}2012. 872–876.

Notes

1   James A. Throgmorton. "Planning as Persuasive Storytelling in a Global-Scale Web of Relationships." *Planning Theory* 2, no. 2 (2003): 125–35; James A. Throgmorton. *Planning as Persuasive Storytelling: The Rhetorical Construction of Chicago's Electric Future.* Chicago: University of Chicago Press, 1996; Merlijn van Hulst. "Storytelling, a Model *of* and a Model *for* Planning." *Planning Theory* 11, no. 3 (2012): 299–318.
2   A detailed recent discussion of this new urban planning interest in narrative is provided by Lieven Ameel. *The Narrative Turn in Urban Planning: Plotting the Helsinki Waterfront.* New York: Routledge, 2021. Cf. also Leonie Sandercock. "From the Campfire to the Computer: An Epistemology of Multiplicity and the Story Turn in Planning." *Multimedia Explorations in Urban Policy and Planning: Beyond the Flatlands.* Ed. Leonie Sandercock, Giovanni Attili. Dordrecht, Heidelberg, New York: Springer, 2010. 17–37; Patsy Healey. "Planning in Relational Space and Time: Responding to New Urban Realities." *A Companion to the City.* Ed. Gary Bridge, Sophie Watson. Oxford: Blackwell, 2000. 517–530.
3   For two influential examples, cf. Robert J. Shiller. *Narrative Economics: How Stories Go Viral and Drive Major Economic Events.* Princeton: Princeton University Press, 2019; Hans Hansen. *Narrative Change: How Changing the Story Can Transform Society, Business, and Ourselves.* New York: Columbia University Press, 2020; for a critical account of the ubiquitous use of the term and its ever-broadening functions in and beyond the humanities and social sciences, cf. Julika Griem and Jo Reichertz, eds. *Mehr*

        als Storytelling. Erzählen in den Geistes- und Sozialwissenschaften. Bielefeld: transcript, 2022.
4   For examples of the dynamic life of stories used in urban revitalization projects, cf. Barbara Buchenau, Jens Martin Gurr, Maria Sulimma, eds. *City Scripts: Narratives of Postindustrial Urban Futures.* Columbus: Ohio State University Press, forthcoming.
5   Cf. Jens Martin Gurr. *Charting Literary Urban Studies: Texts as Models of and for the City.* New York/London: Routledge, 2021. 174–194. Link to open access version: https://doi.org/10.4324/9781003111009.
6   Cf. Ola Söderström, Till Paasche, Francisco Klauser. "Smart Cities as Corporate Storytelling." *City* 18, no. 3 (2014): 307–320.
7   See, e.g., Binay Adhikari, Jianling Li. "Modelling Ambiguity in Urban Planning." *Annals of GIS* 19, no. 3 (2013): 143–152.
8   Cf. the Sustainability Living Labs at Stanford's Doer School of Sustainability and the Urban Living Labs at the Amsterdam Institute for Advanced Metropolitan Solutions.
9   Anthony Ossa-Richardson. *A History of Ambiguity.* Princeton: Princeton University Press, 2019, 2.
10   Albrecht Koschorke. *Fact and Fiction: Elements of a General Theory of Narrative.* Transl. Joel Golb. Berlin/Boston: de Gruyter, 2018 [2012], 349–352 and throughout.
11   The classic discussion of boundary objects is Susan Leigh Star, James Griesemer. "Ecology, 'Translations' and Boundary Objects: Amateurs and Professionals in Berkeley's Museum of Vertebrate Zoology, 1907-39." *Social Studies of Science* 19, no. 3 (1989): 387–420.
12   Antwerp. *Tussen stad en stroom. Het Masterplan Scheldekaaien Antwerpen.* Antwerp: GSA, 2011, 7.
13   Antwerp. *Tussen stad en stroom. Het Masterplan Scheldekaaien Antwerpen.* Antwerp: GSA, 2011, 10.
14   See William Labov, Joshua Waletzky. "Narrative Analysis: Oral Versions of Personal Experience." *Journal of Narrative and Life History* 7, no. 4 (1997) [^{1}1966]: 3–38.
15   See Raina Mäntysalo, Jonna K. Kangasoja, Vesa Kanninen. "The Paradox of Strategic Spatial Planning: A Theoretical Outline

with a View on Finland." *Planning Theory & Practice* 16, no. 2 (2015): 169–183.
16 See Paul Ricœur. *Time and Narrative*. Chicago: University of Chicago Press, 1990 [1984]. 65.
17 The City of New York (Michael R. Bloomberg and Amanda M. Burden). *Vision 2020. New York City Comprehensive Waterfront Plan*. New York: New York City, 2011. 6.
18 The City of New York (Michael R. Bloomberg and Amanda M. Burden). *Vision 2020. New York City Comprehensive Waterfront Plan*. New York: New York City, 2011. 91.
19 Hayden White. *Metahistory: The Historical Imagination in Nineteenth-Century Europe*. Baltimore: Johns Hopkins University Press, 1973. 19.
20 Hayden White. *Metahistory: The Historical Imagination in Nineteenth-Century Europe*. Baltimore: Johns Hopkins University Press, 1973. 9.
21 Olivier Kramsch. "Tropics of Planning Discourse: Stalking the 'Constructive Imaginary' of Selected Urban Planning Histories." *Making the Invisible Visible: A Multicultural Planning History*. Ed. Leonie Sandercock. Berkeley: University of California Press, 1998, 163–183.
22 Mareile Walter. *Making Plans – Telling Stories: Planning in Karlskrona/Sweden 1980–2010*. PhD; thesis, Blekinge Institute of Technology, 2013.
23 A term coined by literary scholar Christoph Bode in 2013. The present outline is strongly indebted to the Introduction to Christoph Bode, Rainer Dietrich. *Future Narratives: Theory, Poetics, and Media-Historical Moment*. Berlin / Boston: de Gruyter, 2013.
24 The City of New York (Bill de Blasio, Dominic Williams, Daniel A. Zarrilli). *OneNYC 2050. Building a Strong and Fair City*. Vol. 1. New York: NYC.GOV, 2019. 6.
25 Merlijn van Hulst. "Storytelling, a Model *of* and a Model *for* Planning." *Planning Theory* 11, no. 3 (2012): 299–318, 300.
26 Bertrand de Jouvenel. *The Art of Conjecture*. Transl. Nikita Lary. New York: Basic Books, 1967. 41ff.

27 Peter Seitel. "Theorizing Genres – Interpreting Works." *New Literary History* 34, no. 2 (2003): 277–279.
28 Helsinki City. *Jätkäsaari osayleiskaava. Selostus*. Helsinki: City Planning, 2008. 8, 60.
29 Cf. Lieven Ameel. "Cities Utopian, Dystopian and Apocalyptic." *Palgrave Handbook of Literature and the City*. Ed. Jeremy Tambling. London: Palgrave, 2016. 785–800.
30 Franco Moretti. *The Way of the World: The Bildungsroman in European Culture*. London: Verso, 1987. 5.
31 Daniel Rabreau. "City Planning." *Encyclopedia of the Enlightenment*. Ed. Michel Delon. Abingdon: Routledge, 2013. 256–262.
32 The City of New York (Michael R. Bloomberg and Amanda M. Burden). *Vision 2020. New York City Comprehensive Waterfront Plan*. New York: New York City, 2011.2.
33 George Lakoff, Mark Johnson. *Metaphors We Live By*. Chicago: Chicago University Press, 2003.
34 Frank Fischer, John Forester, eds. *The Argumentative Turn in Policy Analysis and Planning*. London: Duke University Press, 1993. 11.
35 Kristian Olesen. "Talk to the Hand: Strategic Spatial Planning as Persuasive Storytelling of the Loop City." *European Planning Studies* 25, no. 6 (2017): 978–993.
36 Herbert Stachowiak. *Allgemeine Modelltheorie*. Wien/New York: Springer, 1973. 131–133.
37 Bernd Mahr. "Modelle und ihre Befragbarkeit: Grundlagen einer allgemeinen Modelltheorie." *Erwägen – Wissen – Ethik / Deliberation – Knowledge – Ethics: Forum für Erwägungskultur / Forum for Deliberative Culture* 26, no. 3 (2015): 329–342.
38 Douglass B. Lee. "Requiem for Large-Scale Models." *Journal of the American Institute of Planners* 39, no. 3 (1973): 163–178. Cf. Michael Batty. "Can it Happen Again? Planning Support, Lee's Requiem and the Rise of the Smart Cities Movement." *Environment and Planning B: Planning and Design* 41 (2014): 388–391.
39 Bundesinstitut für Bau-, Stadt- und Raumforschung (BBSR) im Bundesamt für Bauwesen und Raumordnung (BBR), ed. *Von Science-Fiction-Städten lernen. Szenarien für die Stadtplanung*. Bonn: BBSR, 2015.

40 James Phelan. *Experiencing Fiction: Judgements, Progressions, and the Rhetorical Theory of Narrative*. Columbus: Ohio State University Press, 2007. 3.
41 Marie-Laure Ryan. "Narrative." *Routledge Encyclopedia of Narrative Theory*. Ed. David Herman, Manfred Jahn, and Marie-Laure Ryan. Oxford: Routledge, 2005. 344–348, 347.
42 As quoted in Jorma J. Mattila. "Kaikkien aikojen rakennusaalto käynnistyi Helsingissä." *Iltalehti*, September 12, 2008.
43 James A. Throgmorton. *Planning as Persuasive Storytelling: The Rhetorical Construction of Chicago's Electric Future*. Chicago: University of Chicago Press, 1996.
44 Mieke Bal. *Travelling Concepts in the Humanities: A Rough Guide*. Toronto: University of Toronto Press, 2002. 10.
45 Marie-Laure Ryan, Kenneth Foote, Maoz Azaryahu. *Narrating Space, Spatializing Narrative: Where Narrative Theory and Geography Meet*. Columbus: Ohio State University Press, 2016. 139.
46 Helsinki City. *Meri-Helsinki Yleiskaavassa*. Helsinki: City Planning Department, 2013. 18.
47 Richard Sennett. *The Conscience of the Eye: The Design and Social Life of Cities*. New York: W.W. Norton, 1992 [1990]. 190.
48 See for Helsinki's DIY sauna: Susan Bird, Malin Fransberg, Vesa Peipinen. "Hot in Helsinki: Exploring Legal Geographies in a DIY Sauna." *Flinders Law Journal* 18 (2016): 377–397.
49 Aristotle, Longinus, Demetrius. *Aristotle: Poetics. Longinus: On the Sublime. Demetrius: On Style*. Translated by Stephen Halliwell, W. Hamilton Fyfe, Doreen C. Innes, W. Rhys Roberts. Revised by Donald A. Russell. Loeb Classical Library 199. Cambridge, MA: Harvard University Press, 1995. 57.
50 Walter Benjamin. *The Arcades Project*. Trans. Howard Eiland, Kevin McLaughlin. Cambridge, MA: The Belknap Press of Harvard University Press, 1999. 172, 418, 854.
51 Walter Benjamin. *The Arcades Project*. Trans. Howard Eiland, Kevin McLaughlin. Cambridge, MA: The Belknap Press of Harvard University Press, 1999, 418, translation modified; cf. also 4, 390, 392, 418, 462, 841, 854, 879f.
52 See Dieter Hassenpflug. "Once Again: Can Urban Space be Read?" *Reading the City: Developing Urban Hermeneutics/Stadt*

lesen: Beiträge zu einer urbanen Hermeneutik. Ed. Dieter Hassenpflug, Nico Giersig, Bernhard Stratmann. Weimar: Verlag der Bauhaus-Universität, 2011. 49–58, 54.

53 See for instance the pioneering work of Norman Klein on Los Angeles in *The History of Forgetting: Los Angeles and the Erasure of Memory.* London: Verso, 1997/2008.

54 For this example, see David Harvey. "Contested Cities: Social Process and Spatial Form." *The City Reader.* Ed. Richard T. LeGates, Frederic Stout. London/New York: Routledge, ^{4}2000. 225–232. 229.

55 See David Harvey. "Contested Cities: Social Process and Spatial Form." *The City Reader.* Ed. Richard T. LeGates, Frederic Stout. London, New York: Routledge, ^{4}2000. 225–232.

56 See Lieven Ameel. "Emplotting Urban Regeneration: Narrative Strategies in the Case of Kalasatama, Helsinki." *Re-City. Future City – Combining Disciplines.* Ed. Juho Rajaniemi. DATUTOP 34 (2016): 223–241.

57 See Hayden White. "Introduction." *Metahistory: The Historical Imagination in 19th-Century Europe.* Baltimore: Johns Hopkins University Press, 1973.

58 See Arun Jain. "Urban Design Frameworks as a Basis for Development Strategies: A Portland Case Study." (2012). [http://mud-sala.sites.olt.ubc.ca/files/2015/08/Arun-Jain-UDFrameworks-as-Basis-for-Development-Strategies.pdf].

59 Juliane Borosch "Changing the Metonymy: Michigan Central Station and the Face of Detroit." *U.S. American Culture as Popular Culture.* Ed. Astrid Böger, Florian Sedlmeier. American Studies Monograph Series 318. Heidelberg: Universitätsverlag Winter, 2022. 403–423.

60 Juliane Borosch "Changing the Metonymy: Michigan Central Station and the Face of Detroit." *U.S. American Culture as Popular Culture.* Ed. Astrid Böger, Florian Sedlmeier. American Studies Monograph Series 318. Heidelberg: Universitätsverlag Winter, 2022. 403–423.

61 Juliane Borosch "Changing the Metonymy: Michigan Central Station and the Face of Detroit." *U.S. American Culture as Popular Culture.* Ed. Astrid Böger, Florian Sedlmeier. American Stud-

ies Monograph Series 318. Universitätsverlag Winter, 2022. 403–423. 408.
62 Juliane Borosch "Changing the Metonymy: Michigan Central Station and the Face of Detroit." *U.S. American Culture as Popular Culture.* Ed. Astrid Böger, Florian Sedlmeier. American Studies Monograph Series 318. Universitätsverlag Winter, 2022. 403–423. 415, 416.
63 Ford Motor Company. *Michigan Central.* 2022. https://michigancentral.com, last accessed Nov. 12, 2022.
64 Peter Gould. "On Mental Maps." Discussion Paper No. 9. Michigan Interuniversity Community of Mathematical Geographers. Ann Arbor: University of Michigan, 1966; cited in George O. Carney, "Music and Place." *The Sounds of People and Places. A Geography of American Music from Country to Classical and Blues to Bop.* Lanham: Rowman & Littlefield, ^{4}2003, 203–216, 212.
65 For a brief account in English, cf. Martina Löw. "The Intrinsic Logic of Cities: Towards a New Theory on Urbanism." *Urban Research & Practice* 5, no. 3 (2012): 303–315. DOI: 10.1080/17535069.2012.727545.
66 https://www.youtube.com/watch?v=9rR0Awy3R00, accessed August 15, 2022.
67 As Beatrix Busse, Jennifer Smith, Ingo Warnke note, "[t]he city is always also a hard place where exclusion takes place every day. It is important to note that the big-city idea of stylistic self-realization is only one side of the urban narrative. Failure is also part of it." Beatrix Busse, Jennifer Smith, Ingo H. Warnke. "Declaring Places, Placing Declaratives – An Introduction." *Place-Making in the Declarative City.* Ed. Beatrix Busse, Ingo H. Warnke, Jennifer Smith. Berlin/Boston: de Gruyter, 2020. 1–14. 6. https://doi.org/10.1515/9783110634754-001.
68 The subtitle of the poem is literally 'a stream of words of the city'; see Lieven Ameel, "'A Stream of Words' – The Antwerp Quay Poem as Interrogation of Urban Open Form, Polyphony, and Radical Dialogue." *Textual Practice* 36, no. 7 (2021): 1175–1194.
69 Doreen Massey. "On Space and the City." *City Worlds.* Ed. John Allen, Doreen Massey, Steve Pile. London: Routledge, 1999. 151-174, 165.

70 Lieven Ameel. "Towards a Narrative Typology of Urban Planning Narratives for, in, and of Planning in Jätkäsaari, Helsinki." *Urban Design International* 22, no. 4 (2016): 318–330.
71 Jean Hillier. "Deconstructing the Discourse of Planning." *Explorations in Planning Theory*. Ed. Seymour J. Mandelbaum, Luigi Mazza, Robert W. Burchell. New Brunswick: Transaction Publishers, 1996. 289–298, 296.
72 Alexander Sidorkin. "Carnival and Dialogue: Opening New Conversations." *Dialogue as a Means of Collective Communication*. Ed. Bela H. Banathy, Patrick M. Jenlink. New York: Springer, 2005. 277–288. 283.
73 See Sherry J. Arnstein. "A Ladder of Citizen Participation." *Journal of the American Planning Association* 35, no. 4 (1969): 216–224.
74 Christopher Alexander et al. *A Pattern Language: Towns, Buildings, Construction*. New York : Oxford University Press, 1977.
75 Henri Lefebvre. *Éléments de rythmanalyse*. Paris : Éditions Syllepse, 1992. Translation: *Rhythmanalysis: Space, Time and Everyday Life*. London: Continuum, 2004.
76 Derek Attridge. "Rhythm." *The Princeton Encyclopedia of Poetry and Poetics*. Ed. Roland Greene et al. Princeton: Princeton University Press, [4]2012. 1195–1198.
77 Rosemary Gates Winslow. "Meter." *The Princeton Encyclopedia of Poetry and Poetics*. Ed. Roland Greene et al. Princeton: Princeton University Press, [4]2012. 872–876.
78 Paul Fussell. *Poetic Meter & Poetic Form*. London: McGraw, 1979.
79 See Wendell Bell. *Foundations of Futures Studies: History, Purposes, and Knowledge*. London: Routledge, 1997/2003.
80 Dieter Wellershoff. *Literatur und Lustprinzip*. Cologne: Kiepenheuer & Witsch, 1973, 57, our translation; related views have been formulated by Wolfgang Iser in *The Fictive and the Imaginary: Charting Literary Anthropology*. Baltimore: Johns Hopkins University Press, 1993.
81 See Lieven Ameel. "Governing the Future: Perspectives from Literary Studies – Commentary to Jones." *Fennia* 197, no. 1 (2019): 145–148.
82 Cf. BBSR – Bundesinstitut für Bau-, Stadt- und Raumforschung. *Von Science-Fiction-Städten lernen: Szenarien für die*

Stadtplanung. Bonn: BBSR, 2015 [https://www.bbsr.bund.de/BBSR/DE/veroeffentlichungen/sonderveroeffentlichungen/2015/science-fiction-staedte.html]

83 "script." *Oxford English Dictionary Online.* Oxford: Oxford University Press, 2021. <www.oed.com>.

84 Roger C. Schank, Robert P. Abelson. *Scripts, Plans, Goals and Understanding: An Inquiry into Human Knowledge Structures.* Hillsdale: Lawrence Erlbaum, 1977.

85 See Naomi Quinn, Dorothy Holland. "Culture and Cognition." *Cultural Models in Language and Thought.* Ed. Holland, Quinn. Cambridge: Cambridge University Press, 1987. 3–40, as well as James W. Stigler, James Hiebert. *The Learning Gap: Best Ideas from the World's Teachers for Improving Education in the Classroom.* New York: Free Press, 1999.

86 Paul Whitney. "Schemas, Frames, and Scripts in Cognitive Psychology." *International Encyclopedia of the Social & Behavioral Sciences.* Ed. Neil J. Smelser, Paul Baltes. Oxford: Elsevier, 2001. 13522–13526.

87 John H. Gagnon. "Scripts and the Coordination of Sexual Behaviour" [1974]. *The Interpretation of Desire: Essays in the Study of Sexuality.* Ed. Gagnon. Chicago: Chicago University Press, 2004. 59–87. 61.

88 Eric Berne. "Transactional Analysis: A New and Effective Method of Group Therapy." *American Journal of Psychotherapy* 12 (1958): 735–743; Eric Berne. *Transactional Analysis in Psychotherapy: A Systematic Individual and Social Psychiatry.* New York: Grove Press, 1961.

89 See Christopher Alexander, Sara Ishikawa, Murray Silverstein. *A Pattern Language: Towns, Buildings, Construction.* Oxford: Oxford University Press, 1977.

90 See for instance Richard P. Gabriel. *Patterns of Software: Tales from the Software Community.* Oxford: Oxford University Press, 1996.

91 Javier Monclús, Carmen Díez Medina. "Garden Cities and Garden Suburbs (1898–1930)." *Urban Visions: From Planning Culture to Landscape Urbanism.* Ed. Díez Medina, Monclús. Cham: Springer, 2018. 13–22, 19.

92 See Richard Florida. *Cities and the Creative Class*. New York: Routledge, 2005; Richard Florida. *The Rise of the Creative Class: And How It's Transforming Work, Leisure and Everyday Life*. New York: Basic Books, 2002.
93 See Jamie Peck. "Struggling with the Creative Class." *International Journal of Urban and Regional Research* 29, no. 4 (2005): 740–770. 767.
94 See Lieven Ameel. "A *Bildungsroman* for a Waterfront Development: Literary Genre and the Planning Narratives of Jätkäsaari, Helsinki." *Journal of Urban Cultural Studies* 3, no. 2 (2016): 167–187.
95 These disciplines include comparative law, political science, sociology and comparative education, economics and business administration, (critical) urban geography, comparative urban studies, planning studies and architectural research.
96 For a discussion and problematisation of transfers between such "families of nations", cf. Konstantinos Lalenis, Martin de Jong, Virginie Mamadouh. "Families of Nations and Institutional Transplantation." *The Theory and Practice of Institutional Transplantation: Experiences with the Transfer of Policy Institutions*. Ed. de Jong, Mamadouh, Lalenis. Dordrecht: Kluwer Academic Publishers, 2002. 33–52.
97 For influential accounts cf. Jamie Peck, Nik Theodore. *Fast Policy: Experimental Statecraft at the Thresholds of Neoliberalism*. Minneapolis: University of Minnesota Press, 2015.
98 Copenhagenize Design Co. "The 20 Most Bike-Friendly Cities on the Planet, Ranked." 2019. https://copenhagenizeindex.eu.
99 Darran Anderson. *Imaginary Cities*. London: Influx Press, 2015. 208.
100 For accounts of the smart city or the eco-city, see Federico Cugurullo. "The Origin of the Smart City Imaginary: From the Dawn of Modernity to the Eclipse of Reason." *The Routledge Companion to Urban Imaginaries*. Ed. Christoph Lindner, Miriam Meissner. New York: Routledge, 2019. n.p. https://www.taylorfrancis.com/books/e/9781315163956; Simon Joss et al. "The Smart City as Global Discourse: Storylines and Critical Junctures across 27 Cities." *Journal of Urban Technology* 26, no. 1 (2019): 3–34; Ola Söderström et al. "Smart Cities as Corporate

Storytelling." *City* 18, no. 3 (2014): 307–320; Alan Wiig. "IBM's Smart City as a Techno-utopian Policy Mobility." *City* 19, no. 2–3 (2015): 258–273; for the intersections between dominant modes, see Simon Elias Bibri. *Advances in the Leading Paradigms of Urbanism and their Amalgamation: Compact Cities, Eco-Cities, and Data-Driven Smart Cities*. Cham: Springer, 2020.

101 Asian Development Bank. *Green Cities*. Ed. Michael Lindfield, Florian Steinberg. Urban Development Series. Mandaluyong City, Philippines: Asian Development Bank 2012. viii.

102 Northrop Frye. "Varieties of Literary Utopias." *Daedalus* 94, no. 2 (1965). 323–347. 327.

103 Edward E. Hale. *Sybaris and Other Homes*. Boston: Fields, Osgood & Co, 1869. 33.

104 Edward E. Hale. *Sybaris and Other Homes*. Boston: Fields, Osgood & Co, 1869. 41.

105 Northrop Frye. "Varieties of Literary Utopias." *Daedalus* 94, no. 2 (1965): 329.

106 Lewis Mumford. "Utopia, the City and the Machine." *Utopias and Utopian Thought*. Ed. Frank E. Manuel. Boston: Beacon Press, 1975 [1965]. 4.

107 Philip Langdon. *A Better Place to Live: Reshaping the American Suburb*. Amherst: University of Massachusetts Press, 1994. 39.

108 Annette Condello. *The Architecture of Luxury*. Farnham: Ashgate, 2014. 117–118.

109 David Pinder: "Necessary Dreaming: Uses of Utopia in Urban Planning." *The Ashgate Research Companion to Planning Theory*. Ed. Jean Hillier, Patsy Healey. Abingdon: Routledge, 2010. 343–364.

Social Sciences

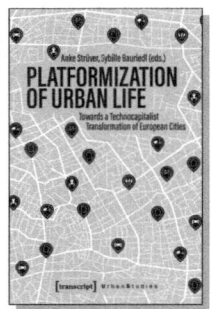

Anke Strüver, Sybille Bauriedl (eds.)
Platformization of Urban Life
Towards a Technocapitalist Transformation of European Cities

September 2022, 304 p., pb.
29,50 € (DE), 978-3-8376-5964-1
E-Book: available as free open access publication
PDF: ISBN 978-3-8394-5964-5

Mihnea Tanasescu
Understanding the Rights of Nature
A Critical Introduction

February 2022, 168 p., pb.
40,00 € (DE), 978-3-8376-5431-8
E-Book: available as free open access publication
PDF: ISBN 978-3-8394-5431-2

Oliver Krüger
**Virtual Immortality –
God, Evolution, and the Singularity
in Post- and Transhumanism**

2021, 356 p., pb., ill.
35,00 € (DE), 978-3-8376-5059-4
E-Book:
PDF: 34,99 € (DE), ISBN 978-3-8394-5059-8

**All print, e-book and open access versions of the titles in our list
are available in our online shop www.transcript-publishing.com**

Social Sciences

Dean Caivano, Sarah Naumes
The Sublime of the Political
Narrative and Autoethnography as Theory

2021, 162 p., hardcover
100,00 € (DE), 978-3-8376-4772-3
E-Book:
PDF: 99,99 € (DE), ISBN 978-3-8394-4772-7

Friederike Landau, Lucas Pohl, Nikolai Roskamm (eds.)
[Un]Grounding
Post-Foundational Geographies

2021, 348 p., pb., col. ill.
50,00 € (DE), 978-3-8376-5073-0
E-Book:
PDF: 49,99 € (DE), ISBN 978-3-8394-5073-4

Andreas de Bruin
Mindfulness and Meditation at University
10 Years of the Munich Model

2021, 216 p., pb.
25,00 € (DE), 978-3-8376-5696-1
E-Book: available as free open access publication
PDF: ISBN 978-3-8394-5696-5

All print, e-book and open access versions of the titles in our list are available in our online shop www.transcript-publishing.com